Seeds of Encouragement

Andrea Sharp

Karol,
May you always
be encouraged in the
love God holds for you!

love,
Andrea Sharp

Seeds of Encouragement
Copyright 2011
By Andrea Sharp
http://www.sharpwomen.com

Cover Design by Dana McBride
Layout Design by Denise Weston

Scripture quotations are taken from the New International Version.
Grand Rapids, MI: Zondervan, 2005

Printed in the United States of America

For more information contact:
Sharp Women
P.O. Box 803
Porterville, CA 93258
559-310-5692
andrea@sharpwomen.com
http://www.sharpwomen.com

Sharp, Andrea
Seeds of Encouragement
ISBN 978-0-615-50600-5
1. Inspiration 2. Encouragement 3. Christian Life
I. Title: Seeds of Encouragement

First Edition 2011

Acknowledgements

To my husband and best friend, Matt who has over, over and over again listened to and read everything I've written! Thank you for always desiring the very best for me. You've made my life complete!

To my three sons, Clay, Jaden and Landon, who inspire me to live life fully and bring such laughter to each day. I am forever grateful for you!

To my family and friends who have been such an encouragement in the fulfillment of this book and in speaking. You bless me abundantly!

To my sister and friend Leisle, who keeps me grounded, makes me laugh and assists me often. I love you dearly!

To Yolanda Harris for her gift of guidance, support and seeing potential in me.

To Denise Weston for her editing and artistic giftedness.

To Crystal Milinich, my neighbor and friend, who was instrumental in the foundation of my dream.

For my sweet sisters and brothers in Christ who have challenged me to grow, learn and stretch. I am so very thankful for you!

To my mentor, friend and encourager, Marnie Swedberg. I so appreciate your belief in me!

Dedication

This book is dedicated to you if you've ever needed to be encouraged and reminded of the love and faithfulness of God. Life happens and because it does we all need some encouragement from time to time. My prayer is that through these stories you will realize how precious you are and that life is a gift. Let's enjoy the journey as we do life together.

Table of Contents

Encouragement…………………………………………….7

Love…………………………………………………..21

Faith……………………………………………….41

Attitude……………………………………………59

Connecting…………………………………………..67

Parenting………………………………………….77

Holidays/Seasons……………………………...…..97

Seeds of Encouragement

Being intentional each day makes
all the difference in how we view
our God-given opportunities.

Encouragement

"Take heart dear one, and do not grow weary.
For the LORD your God is an
ever present help in times of trouble!"

Andrea Sharp

There are no limits to the positive impact we can make in our world.
It takes intentionality on our part, but the effects can be lifelong.
Take time today to share a smile, phone a friend or give aid to
someone in need. The ripple that follows will be life lasting.

Life Happens

One sunny summer afternoon I was visiting a local fast food restaurant in town with my oldest son and nephew.

While we were there, we ran into a lovely lady who was ordering her dinner. She was inside talking with some friends when another lady (me) backed into her car, scraping off plenty of paint and leaving a sizeable scratch.

Not knowing whose car it was, I sheepishly ventured into the restaurant and began inquiring of patrons to find out who drove that particular make and model. After asking the staff and several groups of those eating, I finally came across the owner. Humbly, I explained that I had backed into her vehicle in the parking lot. She abruptly ended her conversation with her friends and we both walked outside to survey the damage. I didn't know what to say. "I'm sorry" wasn't going to change the obvious, but it was a start. I didn't know if she would scream or throw a fit. She just looked at her bumper and with slumped shoulders breathed a sad kind of sigh. I thought selfishly to myself, "Thank God she's not a scene-maker."

After exchanging names, addresses and insurance information, our conversation changed. She asked about my boys in the car and commented that they were waiting patiently. We began discussing family and life changes. We were similar in age and both worked in education. Through our parking lot talk I learned this woman was facing a great deal of pain and loss. I couldn't fix her car–that was my insurance company's job–but I would remind her of the unfailing love and devotion of her heavenly Father. At times we all need to be reminded of the availability of our gracious God and the help He offers. We spoke some more, cried, prayed and then went our separate ways.

Seeds of Encouragement

In this life no one enjoys trouble or heartache. But to be sure, we will all experience it sooner or later. Sometimes I get so wrapped up in the bountiful blessing of God that I forget the pitfalls of this earth. Jesus himself said we would experience trouble. In John 16:33 Jesus says, "In this world you will have trouble. But take heart! I have overcome the world." Are not all situations and circumstances filtered through His fingertips? As a sword is refined in the blazing furnace to make it unbreakable, so we too are refined through hardship to mature and strengthen us. God indeed has a plan for our good and for His glory in troublesome times.

One night my husband and I were watching TV. We were channel flipping and came across a program that was filmed in Asia. In it, a man was demonstrating the process of making a modern-day sword the old fashioned way. He began with a long piece of rectangular–shaped steel. He then put the piece of steel into a fiery hot furnace. Just before the steel began to melt, the swordsman took it out of the fire and began hammering it into the shape of a sword. Then he placed it into a liquid to cool for just a few seconds, quenching the heat.

Over and over, he repeated this same process: fire, pounding, shaping, quenching; fire, pounding, shaping, quenching. When he was done, the man then placed the sword into a vice which held it in place. Another man put a high-powered automatic gun on a stand pointed directly at the sword. The point of this demonstration was to test how much damage would be done to the sword when shot with a high-speed bullet. Much to our surprise, the bullet ricocheted off the sword and left only a scratch.

Our lives are sometimes like that sword. In any given day, the bullets of life can come hard and fast. It's through those difficult times that we are stretched, molded and more conformed into the image of Jesus Christ. Without these, we're simply not as strong and refined as God wants us to be. With the power of God working in our lives, we will gain strength and endurance for daily living. Therefore take heart dear one, and do not grow weary. Matthew 11:28 says, "Come to me, all who are weary and burdened, and I will give you rest."

Life happens, you can be sure, but our lives are in the Master's hands and He knows what we face each day. We can trust Him fully to carry us through. And just like the lovely lady I bumped into, He gives us each other to be a source of comfort and love along our life's journey.

Seeds of Encouragement

In any given day the bullets of life can come hard and fast. It's through those times of difficulties that we are stretched, molded and more conformed into the image of Jesus Christ. As life happens, do not grow weary. God gives us each other to be a source of comfort and love along our journey.

"Try not to become a man of success but a man of value."
Albert Einstein

Seize the Day

"Mom, you're like the oldest mom in the world!" my youngest son Landon said one day while we were driving down the road. I said, "Goodness, Landon, not really." "Well, for short people, you're like the oldest mom," he replied. My second son, Jaden, soon piped in, "Landon, girls don't like hearing that they're old." He then sighed and said, "She's the mom, so it's ok she's old."

I realize the years are catching up with me, but I don't believe I'm at the stage of 'being set out to pasture' quite yet. I have wondered before though, as two separate women have asked me if I was my children's grandma. "You've got to be kidding me!" I thought. I know I probably need a new 'do and usually, I am running around looking half ragged anyway, but a grandmother??? Please!!

Recently, I was asked to sing the "Mom's Song" at a church luncheon in Visalia for the "Prime Timers," a group of retirees. (Now I'm wondering if they think I am a 'prime timer' too!) Anyway, I was speaking with the coordinator on the phone and she made a comment about those in her group who were questioning their usefulness and purpose. My heart just melted for them. After being a caregiver for the elderly for seven years, God has grown in me a heart of compassion for those in the sunset years of life. I have watched my in-laws struggle in trying to find their purpose as they age. As I always tell Dad (my father-in-law), if you're still breathing, God has an ordained purpose for you.

As I write this article, I am at Hartland Christian Camp, which is located in the gorgeous Sequoia National Forest. I'm sitting under the shade of a group of towering redwoods and a hint of fall is in the air. There is an older lady making her way along the sidewalk. As she pushes her walker, it is evident she has severe osteoporosis in her back. Her gait is slow and careful. But her spirit is still that of a young woman, as she begins hollering to the younger women, "I want to be there when you go on those adventures on the zip line and extreme swing!" What an example! She may not be able to embark on that journey herself, but she doesn't want to miss sharing in it. Oh, how that blesses me!

When we're young, we tend to find our purpose in our spouse, children, career or social outlets. But as we age, sometimes those purposes diminish and we're left wondering, "What on earth am I here for?"

The answer is simple: to know God and bring Him glory. That's the summation of our life purpose. God created us in our mother's womb. There is not another person on the face of the earth who has lived, is living, or will live, that shares our exact fingerprints or DNA. You are truly 'one of a kind'. Psalm 139:13-14 says, "For you created my inmost being; you knit me together in my mother's womb. I praise you because I am fearfully and wonderfully made; your works are wonderful, I know that full well."

Beloved, our job on this earth, at whatever season we're in, is to "Love the Lord your God with all your heart, soul and mind," (Matthew 22:37) and to bring glory to Him through our actions and attitudes. "In the same way, let your light shine before men, that they may see your good deeds and praise your Father in heaven." (Matthew 5:16)

If you're still breathing, this is your time to shine for the King of kings! The time is now to impact your world for Jesus Christ. Make a phone call, write a letter or email, hug your spouse, and love on your children, grandchildren, neighbors and friends. Bake some cookies, make a cake, mow a neighbor's lawn or put their trash bin out for pickup. "And whatever you do, whether in word or deed, do it all in the name of the Lord Jesus, giving thanks to God the Father through him." (Colossians 3:17) Seize this day for God and in doing so, may the whole world know, Jesus loves you so!!

Seeds of Encouragement

"What on earth am I here for?"
The answer is simple: to know God and bring Him glory.
That's the summation of our life purpose.

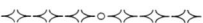

"The way to gain a good reputation is to endeavor to be what you desire to appear."

Socrates

Let Your Light Shine

Did you know that God has provided each of His children with gifts and talents? The purpose of these is to bring Him glory and to show the world the love of Jesus.

In our household there are seven of us, ranging in age from 5 to 90. It can get quite chaotic at times with kids playing and our dog Taylor barking. There's rarely a dull moment. But in the noise and busyness, we all try to remember our household theme - "to show others Jesus." When the doorbell rings or the boys are playing with the neighborhood kids, we try to remind each other of this. Our lives are just a moment in time and we want to make them count for God.

In each of our lifetimes it is said we will directly or indirectly influence approximately 10,000 people. When I ponder the impact of that I am astounded at the possibilities. Our family alone will influence about 70,000 people. That is more than the size of my town of Porterville. What am I doing with "my sphere of influence?" Am I using the gifts and talents God has given me to share the good news of Jesus? Do my neighbors and friends know God better because they know me?

In Rick Warren's bestselling book, *The Purpose Driven Life*, he states, "Nothing matters more than knowing God's purposes for your life, and nothing can compensate for not knowing them." God made each of us unique and with that He has given us strengths and talents to use in serving Him and to bless us.

In determining the gift or gifts God has blessed you with it is helpful to ask yourself:

*What is my passion, what do I enjoy?

Seeds of Encouragement

*What have others affirmed in me?
*What do I have experience or training in?

Many times experiences of the past prepare us for the situations we will encounter in the future. Jobs we've held, training, and education are all tools God can use to lead us down the path He has for us. In being a caregiver for my in-laws, my teenage job as a nurse's aide has come in handy more times than I can count.

When we're living our God-given purpose and fulfilling the life God has called us to we will experience abundant life. The key to knowing our purpose and growing in it is to "submit, seek and serve". First, we have to submit our lives to God on a daily basis. Before being crucified Jesus prayed to His Father in Matthew 26:39, "Yet not as I will, but as you will." Jesus led by example that it's not about us, but about God alone.

Secondly, we must seek God each day through prayer and Bible study. As we submit to God and seek Him, He will reveal His will for us. Lastly, we must be willing to serve others with our talents and gifts. The Bible says in Matthew 5:16, "Let your light shine before men that they may see your good deeds and praise your Father in heaven." By using our God-given gifts people get a better glimpse of who God really is and the love He has for each one of us.

We can trust God fully to lead us on the course He has for us. Our job is to trust and obey. For truly there's no other way to joyfully live the abundant life God has for each one of His children.

Seeds of Encouragement

Many times experiences in our past prepare us for situations we'll encounter in the future. God can use these in our lives to reveal our gifts and talents, resulting in living our God-given purpose and fulfilling the life He has planned for us.

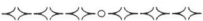

"Every great dream begins with a dreamer. Always remember,
you have within you the strength, the patience,
and the passion to reach for the stars to change the world."
Harriet Tubman

Patience with Porthos

I'm nuts about my husband, Matt! He's been my best friend for 25 years. Within the first week of meeting him I was smitten. After almost 22 years of marriage my heart still leaps for joy when he comes home.

It was with these heart strings that I decided to bless him for his birthday with a new puppy. He'd wanted a Beagle puppy for some time. The opportunity arose to acquire one and I jumped on it.

Making a decision with my heart instead of engaging my brain beforehand has gotten me into pickles more times than I would like to admit. This time was no different. The Bible states in Jeremiah 17:9, "The heart is deceitful above all things and beyond cure. Who can understand it?" I should've read this verse before getting Porthos.

Porthos was by far the cutest of the litter. He's a Lilac Beagle; called this for his unique brown and white coloring and hazel eyes. He is absolutely adorable with his droopy long ears and sad eyes. He was also the runt of the litter, so I was immediately drawn to his neediness and knew my family would be his rescue.

Within two months I was looking for a new home for Porthos. He had a high pitched bark that was absolutely shocking the first time I heard it. My blood pressure skyrocketed and so did the noise in the house, because we couldn't hear each other speak. My husband suggested getting a shock collar. "No way!" I emphatically announced, "We can't shock him into submission!" Three days later I called Matt at work. "Don't come home until you have a shock collar with you!" "I thought you didn't want to get one." Matt said. "That was before YOUR dog was making me crazy!" I replied.

Seeds of Encouragement

For his safety as a puppy, our vet suggested not to let him roam free around the house. Good advice. We put a leash on him and where we walked, he walked. While I would make dinner, I would put his leash under the leg of our ottoman. He ate it. I moved him to the kitchen table. He ate that. We put him in our bathroom (it had no furniture to eat) while we were at church. We came home to find he'd eaten the baseboard and wall. "That's it!!" I exclaimed, "We've got to find a new home for Porthos." Within 3 days he was relocated to a new family. My sweet husband was crushed, but once again our house was peaceful! "Aaahh, yes", I said one evening, "See now we can relax without wondering what Porthos is up to."

We knew it was best but Porthos was missed, especially by Matt and our son Landon. Each night Landon would pray that Porthos would come home. I should have known God would be tender towards this precious, heartfelt prayer of a little one. Two months later Porthos was back. Matt and Landon were elated! Truthfully speaking I was too! Even though he drives me crazy I genuinely love and care for Porthos. We were determined to make it work.

Regretfully, determination doesn't always suffice. Hard work, tremendous patience and much grey hair has gone into the training of Porthos. He's eaten clothes, shoes, and carpet. We put him outside and he digs holes beside every tree he can find. He's been neutered, shock-collared, muzzled, praised, redirected and even given a stern talking to. We're all learning about patience, forbearance and unconditional love. Believe it or not, even with everything he's done, I still find him adorable!

I guess God feels that same way about me. Even with my countless mistakes and sins, He still finds me adorable! How that is possible, I'll never know this side of heaven. But when I see

Jesus' precious smile someday, I will fully know, just as I have been fully known.

So be encouraged this new year; wherever you are, whatever you've done, the love of God stands firm. He will always love and adore you! Nothing we do or have done will EVER change that! 2 Peter 3:9 says, "The Lord is not slow in keeping his promise, as some understand slowness. He is patient with you, not wanting anyone to perish, but EVERYONE to come to repentance." (Emphasis mine) Just like our patience with Porthos, God is ever patient with us. Praise God for that!

Seeds of Encouragement

Oh, how I'm thankful for God's relentless patience! I've been in the pit, taken the road most traveled and been in more sticky spots than I care to remember. But God has been faithful to this former weak willed girl and I am so tremendously grateful for that! God is patient with you too! He loves you and adores you so much! The next time you're questioning His fortitude, just read 2 Peter 3:9. His love and faithfulness endures forever.

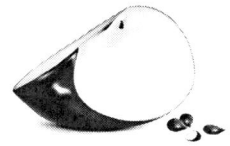

Love

"And now these three remain:
faith, hope and love.
But the greatest of these is love."
1 Corinthians 13:13

Why does God desire a relationship with me? I've asked myself
that question countless times. After all, God certainly doesn't need
me. He has the world at His finger tips and can have anything He
wants. But He wants time and attention from me. How very
humbled I am by that fact! Like a parent feels adoration for their
child, so God feels the same way about us. How He loves to spend
time with us! Choose this day to sit in His presence and to relish in
His complete and pure love for you. It will not only change your
day, it will change your life!

He Loves Me, He Loves Me Still

Earlier this week I stepped outside into my front yard to take our dog Taylor for a bathroom break. I looked up and saw one of my neighbors and her boys walking across the street. We all stopped under a shade tree and began to chat about school, the heat and families. One of her children began to inquire about the saying 'if you talk the talk, you need to walk the walk'. He wanted to know what it meant. Curious question I thought, coming from a ten year old. But knowing this sweet soul for the past six years has taught me that he has depth beyond his years, and a heart that desires what is good and true. His mom explained the metaphor and the boys went on playing.

Afterwards the Lord began to inquire in my own heart, "Andrea, do your talk and walk match? Do you follow what you teach your children - to love others and pray for those who persecute them?" Strangely enough, in the last few days our family has had the wonderful opportunity to do just that. To be honest, we were missing the mark of what God desires for us.

You see, a family member's credit card was stolen and the fraudulent charges were excessive. We completed a police report and a court date was set. This whole situation has caused much anger and grief. Our initial response was typical. Why in the world would someone take advantage like this? Why can't people just be nice? Our questions simply led to more irritation and stress.

The Lord in His sweetness began to whisper, "Come to me all who are weary and burdened and I will give you rest." We stopped griping and began praying. When we finished the situation was still there, but we had a different perspective. We were reminded that there's no power without prayer and God was indeed walking us through this journey. But God wasn't finished with us yet. As the neighbor boy reminded me, I do indeed need to walk the talk I profess. Matthew 5:44 says, "But I tell you: Love your enemies and pray for those who persecute you." In my selfishness, I didn't want to pray for the offender and I certainly didn't want to love him. But God never asked if I wanted to. His directions were clear and concise: pray for and love your enemies. Our family made a commitment to do just that.

Each night we gather for prayer and ask our boys if they have any special prayer requests. They remember the commitment we made and pray for the person who stole from us. One of my sons said, "Lord, please let him come to know you as LORD and Savior, and help him to stop stealing." As he prayed I realized I am no better than the thief that has caused us so much stress.

Where would I be without the redeeming work of God in my own life? Without the blood of Jesus covering my sins, I would not have His grace and forgiveness. He took my place (and yours) on that cross. Praise God for His indescribable gift! We all fail in our daily walk in this life, but isn't it good to know that our God still loves us and calls us His own?

As I've said before, the Lord desires a personal relationship with each one of us. That means EVERYONE, no matter our past, or even our present. There's nothing in the Bible that teaches us to get our lives straight and then come to God. Instead, Jesus said in Matthew 9:13, "For I have not come to call the righteous, but sinners." We are all sinners; none of us are righteous. But God in His mercy still chooses to have a friendship with us.

When Jesus walked on the earth, He didn't hang out with the religious leaders, but with the sinners and those who were sick and lame. He came to reveal the very heart of God, a God who is loving, generous and forgiving.

Seeds of Encouragement

How can He still love and forgive me when He knows me inside and out; my thoughts, actions and motives? As a child of God I still struggle with issues like selfishness and laziness. You can bet if there's one cookie left, I'm going to want it. Right now, my very favorite pie is in our refrigerator. I told my husband just this morning, "There's one piece of MY pie left. Be sure to leave it for me." He simply mumbled to himself.

Also, I know for good health I need to exercise regularly. I have absolutely no desire to work out. I sit on my couch eating Rocky Road ice cream. As I'm enjoying the sweetness of chocolate I query the Lord as to why I can't be naturally thin like my sister. You know, that's the great and completely awesome miracle of our God. He knows us inside and out, our defects, and our imperfections. Despite everything He loves us. He loves us still. Do you know that today? Do you have that fact wrapped around your soul? Do you realize that His love is not based on works? It is NOT conditional and it is FOREVER!

As my family is learning to pray for and love those who meant us harm, let me encourage you to acknowledge with a grateful heart the love and forgiveness of our gracious God. Regardless of where you are today, He loves you. He loves you still.

Seeds of Encouragement

Negative circumstances in our lives rarely change overnight. The key to endurance is remembering who God is and how He loves us. That might not change the situation, but it will definitely change our perspective.

"A good deed is never lost: he who sows courtesy reaps friendship; he who plants kindness gathers love."

Saint Basil

Love Means Always Having to Say You're Sorry

Recently, as my family gathered over Mom's vegetarian lasagna, hot buttery rolls and a large green salad, three generations began lively conversation about politics, elections and football. The topic of apologizing came up and the conversation grew even livelier.

Now anyone who knows me well knows that I have a certain proclivity for apologizing a lot. If my boys have had an issue at school, I'll say, "Honey, I'm sorry that happened." If the boys don't obey their dad, I'll say, "Ooh, I'm sorry sweetie." If I see a friend and they tell me of some problem in their life, I'll simply apologize for them having to deal with that issue. I realize I drive people nuts by doing this. But truly, I AM SORRY! I feel so bad for people and the situations they face that I just apologize for it.

Even though my family knows me better than anyone, they don't understand me and my apologetic ways. My cousin told us about a scenario at work and I felt bad for him, so I said....you guessed it, "I'm sorry." This brought up a question I have heard so often.. "Why are you sorry Andrea? You didn't have anything to do with it." Then the flood of inquiries came. "Why do you always say you're sorry? She'll say she sorry to everyone! Why do you do that? I just shrugged and said, "I don't know, I feel bad for people."

Our conversation continued and we began discussing why it's so hard for most people to apologize when they've done something wrong either intentionally or unintentionally. We had a good debate on whether a person should apologize when they hadn't 'meant' to harm another person.

A case in point is a couple of brothers I know. They've been best friends since birth and do many things together. This may be confusing, but stay with me. One brother said something to the other's wife that was true, but nevertheless, didn't need to be said. Now, brother two won't speak to brother one until he apologizes. Heartache has ensued for both families, immediate and extended.

Romans 12:18 states, "If it is possible, as far as it depends on you, live at peace with everyone." What an exhortation for us all! If it's up to us, be at peace with EVERYONE!

I don't know about you, but God has been increasingly laying this fact upon my heart - TIME IS SHORT!! Beloved, stubbornness doesn't produce anything positive. Over time it can fester inside of us, causing stress, ulcers and depression. Our enemy seeks "to kill and steal and destroy." Jesus said, "I have come that they may have life, and have it to the full." John 10:10 (NIV) Satan desires to kill our joy, steal our relationships and destroy our health. God desires just the opposite: a life full of abundant joy, healthy relationships and less stress.

In the 1970's movie *Love Story*, Ali McGraw makes the infamous statement, "Love means never having to say you're sorry." No offense to Ali, but she was dead wrong! God desires for us to humble our hearts, get rid of our 'stiff necks' and treat others as we want to be treated.

That means apologizing when we've hurt someone, whether we meant to or not. Proverbs 16:18 states, "Pride goes before destruction, a haughty spirit before a fall." It's pride that keeps us from apologizing, so we have to recognize it for what it is.

When my sweet husband is avoiding a situation and doesn't want to deal with it, I'll say to him, "Now honey, you've just got to take this bull by the horns and deal with it." He loves to hear that!! It's not music to his ears, but it's the truth.

Seeds of Encouragement

Sweet friends, I encourage you today if you need to make an apology, to 'just grab the bull by the horns and deal with it.' A sincere apology takes less than sixty seconds. It doesn't cost us a penny and causes no pain to our bodies. The results will generally be positive, can potentially bring real healing and have life-changing results. You can do it!!

With Thanksgiving over and Christmas coming soon, there's no better time to build bridges. James 4:10 says, "Humble yourselves before the Lord, and he will lift you up." What an awesome promise! If we humble ourselves and get rid of our stiff necks, then Jesus Himself will lift us up. Glory! It doesn't get better than that.

During this beautiful Thanksgiving season, I am truly thankful for you. God has made you in His likeness. He loves and adores you so very much!!

Seeds of Encouragement

"If it's possible, as far as it depends on you, live at peace with everyone." Romans 12:18 A sincere apology takes less than a minute, costs us nothing and causes no physical pain. The results potentially bring real healing and can have life changing results.

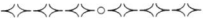

"It is hard to fail, but it is worse never to have tried to succeed."
Theodore Roosevelt

Debt of Honor

Henry Adams said, "A teacher affects eternity: she can never tell where her influence stops."

I'm a fourth generation teacher. I never wanted to teach. I desired a position with more prestige, not to mention more money. I defaulted into an education degree because I simply couldn't figure out what prestigious position I wanted. But I knew it was out there and I was going to find it.

One day I found myself out of work and needing a job. I wondered how Matt and I would make ends meet. "Aha!" I thought, "I can substitute teach." I would make the sacrifice to substitute until I could find a 'real' job. My first job was first grade: 30 little ones with runny noses, untied shoelaces and grubby faces. It seemed I spent most of the day trying to get them to stay focused and stay in their seats. I tied more shoestrings that day than I had in my entire life!

After lunch recess, one small cherub-faced boy walked up and handed me a crumpled bouquet of green weeds and a yellow wildflower. His hands were grungy and dirty. He was missing his two front teeth. He smiled sweetly and in a voice barely more than a whisper said, "These are for you." I almost cried. This boy had only met me 3 hours earlier, yet he thought I was special enough to bring me flowers. In that moment my life and heart were changed. That day of substituting made me feel more alive than any other job I had in the past.

I burst through the door at home and almost screamed at Matt, "I want to teach!" No more corporate jobs for me! I knew teaching was in my blood.

Seeds of Encouragement

The woman who engrained in me the philosophy that teaching was so much more than simply instructing is my mom. I attended the same school where my mom taught kindergarten. We lived in a small farming community of 600 people in northern Oklahoma. Teachers were paid practically nothing.

When I was in second grade, a kindergartner, whom I'll call Ashley, and who had cerebral palsy, enrolled in Mom's class,. She could not walk, feed herself or use the restroom independently. There was no such thing as instructional aides or resource assistance of any kind at that time. Our town didn't have a doctor, much less a physical therapist. Mom was well before her time with the concept of 'no child left behind'. As a teacher, Mom felt there was no reason Ashley couldn't participate in school just like the rest of the class. Ashley's quick wit met my Mom's and they soon formed a special bond.

Ashley's doctors told her parents she would need physical therapy three times daily to improve muscle strength, flexibility and coordination. With those services not available in our town, Mom decided to take on this task. Each morning before class, during lunch and again after school Mom would recruit another teacher and 2 students (generally me and a friend). In sequence, we would gingerly move Ashley's arms and legs, rotating, straightening, and bending. Ashley endured this daily ritual like a champion. Mom would make silly remarks that kept Ashley laughing and distracted. During this time Ashley and Mom's love and devotion for each other continued to grow.

Through this experience I quickly learned that teaching was so much more than simply instructing. It's thinking outside the box, being innovative, motivating and it's sometimes heartbreaking. Time moved forward and Ashley grew. She graduated from high school at the top of her class and went on to graduate from Oklahoma University. She is now married and lives in Oklahoma.

In 42 years of teaching, Mom has taught elementary, junior high, special education and college students. The Lord only knows how many total students she's impacted and influenced. Just like Henry Adams said, she's affected eternity.

Yesterday, Mom retired from Porterville College. Her legacy will continue through programs she instituted and the people she has impacted. I spoke with a former student mom helped during her tenure at Porterville College. He called her "an angel walking here on earth" and said that she makes the impossible possible with her die-hard spirit.

Where would we be without teachers like her? Instructing, loving, and making the impossible possible. "Limitations" is not a part of most teacher's vocabulary.

Mom, today others and I salute you! In my debt of honor, may I continue the passion of teaching, loving and influencing you've set forth in my heart.

Seeds of Encouragement

Teaching is so much more than simply instructing. It's thinking outside the box, being innovative, motivating and it's sometimes heartbreaking. Teaching is an incredible calling! Three cheers for sacrificial and influential teachers who affect so many lives!!

"Success is the sum of small efforts, repeated day in and day out."
Robert Collier
"Courage isn't the absence of fear; it's the dealing with it."
Randall "Tex" Cobb

Bridging the Gap

When trying to mesh the young with the old,

How do we do it? How do we mold

The young with receptive hearts and the old with willing minds,

To listen, laugh and learn, to instruct, build and bind?

There's so much to learn, there's so much to teach,

The young with the old is not beyond reach.

We need them and they need us;

It's really simple, what's all the fuss?

When we remember that someday we too

Will walk in their places; we'll be in their shoes.

Our day is coming and not too far off,

We will be the older ones and hearing the youngsters scoff.

So bridge the gap, the young with the old.

Take time for each other, joining hearts to hold.

Andrea Sharp

Caring Can Be Hard

The past six years haven't always worked out as we had planned. When my granddad moved in with us seven years ago the arrangement was much like having a roommate. He was fairly independent and still able to participate in daily activities. We asked him to come and live with us because his beloved wife of 63 years was in a nursing home and deteriorating quickly. He was lonely without her, so we thought the company of our two rambunctious toddlers would be just what he needed.

Much to our dismay, a week after he moved in, he had his fifth heart attack. The doctors looked at his heart, the damage it had suffered, and told us that he was terminal. Our fun-loving addition to our family had one to two months to live.

Soon the hospital called and wanted to arrange hospice services. I felt as if the room was spinning. In one week our lives metamorphosed from having a family roommate to full-time terminal care. Nothing in my life could have prepared me for this season.

While Granddad was still recuperating in the hospital, and on his birthday, my grandma died. There was no time to mourn Grandma because the care for Granddad was so intense. Being a wife, mother, teacher and caregiver was incredibly taxing and lonely. My husband and I were on our own as far as Granddad's care was concerned. Hospice came a few times a week, but the rest was left to us. Many people offered their sympathies, but few actually took action to assist us. The days and nights became a blur. Sometimes we wondered how we would survive this, but our faith was strong and day by day the strength we required was there.

Exactly two months after Grandma died, Granddad went to be with her. For the first time I was able to weep over both of them.

Seeds of Encouragement

Waves of exhaustion, relief and sadness spilled over me. Sometimes at night I would find myself lying on the floor of Granddad's room, crying. I mourned over lost expectations and the way I thought things would be. Guilt washed over me as I wondered if I should have done things differently.

Today I find myself in those same uncomfortable shoes of the past. My in-laws moved in with us five years ago. At the time, their health wasn't good and they were frail. They were 85 and 83 years old, and our sons were 7, 3, and 1. We never anticipated that five years later we would still be caring for both young and old.

This road we've chosen has been filled with struggles and tears. My mother and father-in-law's needs have only increased with each passing year. Days have not been easy. Any mother knows with three little ones there is rarely a down moment, a chance to just stop and catch your breath. It seems with caring for our in-laws and little ones there is always someone in need. The struggle to manage it all has been enormous.

Many times I've found myself frustrated and tired at the end of the day, wondering if I've got what it takes to continue. As my in-laws aged, choices for alternate living arrangements lessened. Should we even ponder a care facility, when we've made a commitment to them? How would we afford outside care? Would it break their hearts at the mere mention of another home?

There was just no way around the guilt we felt. We knew our growing boys needed more time, but so did Mom and Dad. We prayed. We cried. We prayed some more. We found ourselves at a precipice. Which direction should we go? Caring can be hard.

This weekend Mom and Dad are moving into a full-time care home. We have all started the process of mourning this move. We know it's necessary and that they need more help than we can give. But somehow I always thought they would die peacefully in their sleep in the same bed they have shared for almost seventy years. Life doesn't always happen like we plan. But looking back I am keenly aware that the blessings we have received from this journey far outweigh the struggles.

Our boys have learned a great deal of compassion as they have watched their dad and I lovingly care for the needs of their grandparents. We have benefited from the wisdom of these Depression-era survivors, about things ranging from financial sense to maintaining a solid marriage. It's our hope that we will take these morsels of knowledge and infuse them into our daily living, ultimately affecting our neighborhood and towns in a positive manner. Sowing seeds of care is not easy sometimes, but the rewards are real. Someday when the wounds are not so fresh, we will remember these times and hold them dear.

Seeds of Encouragement

Life doesn't always happen like we plan. Looking back I am keenly aware that the blessings we have received from this journey far outweigh the struggles. Whatever you're facing, remember you're not alone. Seek wisdom from God through prayer and Bible reading. Connect with friends and family who support and encourage you along the way. We're not islands, we need each other.

Sandwiched

We never know how life will change,
Or what might come to pass.
We assume each day will remain the same,
In our houses made of glass.

One day Granddad moved in with us,
And went about life as he willed.
Not knowing that in just five short days,
Would begin the end of a life fulfilled.

The prognosis for him was terminal
With one to two months to live.
Hospice care soon became our norm
We wondered if we had anything left to give.

Days and weeks seemed to run together,
And exhaustion took on new meaning.
Our family became closer and stronger
We clung to the One on whom we'd been leaning.

Soon Granddad was with our Savior and Lord
And recovery for us began.
The time between passed by so fast,
Soon we were caregivers again.

Seeds of Encouragement

Our aging parents needed care,
And transition was upon us.
With three small boys bustling here and there,
Oh, how will we juggle the ruckus?

Now in all there are seven of us,
Ages one to eighty-five.
The balancing act we face is tremendous
As each day for the best we strive

How do we manage, how do we cope,
Whose cry do we answer first?
Are we meeting the needs of all involved?
In Godly love and not angry bursts?

We need you God on this lonely trail,
We're sandwiched in between.
A generation between the young and old
On your strength we all will lean.

Andrea Sharp

The Sandwich Generation is growing every day. As the Baby Boomers age, more and more of us will be caring for both young and old. It's not a position most people would choose for themselves or their families. Just how can we balance the needs of both? One day and one step at a time, being patient with ourselves and with others. It's a huge learning curve and not one that can be attained overnight. So, take time to breath, be good to you and seek the assistance of others.

Faith

*"Faith isn't the ability to believe long and far
into the misty future.
It's simply taking God at His Word
and taking the next step."*
Joni Erickson Tada

Seeds of Encouragement

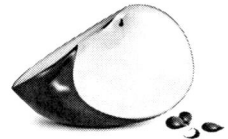

*"Now faith is confidence in what we hope for
and assurance about what we do not see."*

Hebrews 11:1

MUD and GUNK

This weekend my family and I decided to do some much needed yard work. The air was cool and motivation was high (at least on my part). Plants were overgrown and some had a lot of dead underbrush that needed be pulled out of the ground. I pulled and clipped, while the boys raked and threw the piles into our green trash bin.

When we finished that project the boys eagerly joined the street football game they had so sacrificially postponed until we were done. I decided to continue with my fall cleaning by sweeping grass and sand that had collected on our street, right next to our sidewalk curb. Sweeping sand is not the brightest idea I've ever had. I've pushed cars that were easier to move than the sand!

I swept what little I had collected into a dustpan and realized this plan wasn't going to work. So...I got a hose and began spraying the sand towards the gutter. The sand quickly became much thicker and heavier than before. I was determined though; that sand was going down the drain if it took me all evening (and that it did).

The process was very slow. Moving the mud and gunk out of the gutter and into the drain took me forever. I would spray a section and watch it move a teensy way down the street, then spray another section, over and over. It was dark by the time I finished. How could a simple job turn into such a long and arduous task?

As I was talking with the Lord this morning, I prayed for God to remove the gunk of sin from my life and replace my heart with Him instead. Eureka! It seemed like God said to me, "Andrea, your heart is just like that sandy mud and gunk out there. Every day you need to ask me to empty your sinful nature out of your heart and replace it with me."

Seeds of Encouragement

According to Webster's Dictionary, gunk is described as a filthy, sticky or greasy matter. That pretty much represents our hearts when we're not filled with the Holy Spirit. "What a wretched man I am! Who will rescue me from this body of death? Thanks be to God - through Jesus Christ our Lord!" the apostle Paul declares in Romans 7:24-25.

Glory to God in the highest! For our power for effective living does not come from us, but from the power of the Holy Spirit. Galatians 5:22-23 says, "But the fruit of the Spirit is love, joy, peace, patience, kindness, goodness, faithfulness, gentleness and self control. Against such things there is no law."

What a beautiful fruitful picture of what we can show to a needy world. Everyone around us benefits when we express the fruit of the Holy Spirit. What spouse, child, family member or neighbor wouldn't benefit greatly from seeing these same aspects in our daily lives? Would more people be drawn to God? I think so. When His children exhibit 'fruit' attributes that are so opposite of the ever prevalent 'me' culture, the world will take notice.

Praise be to God because He is the ultimate example of expressing these. I am so thankful God is patient and full of self control when I am having a bad day. Oh, the love Jesus showed for us when He willingly gave up His rights to die an ugly death for our gain. John 3:16 states, "God so loved the world that he gave his one and only son, that WHOEVER believes in him shall not perish but have eternal life." (Emphasis mine)

In Matthew, chapter 7, Jesus is teaching about fruit in people's lives. It says in verses 16 and 20, "By their fruit you will recognize them." John 15:16 states, "You did not choose me, but I chose you and appointed you to go and bear fruit - fruit that will last."

Seeds of Encouragement

As I said earlier, we can't "go and bear fruit" on our own power. It comes only from the Holy Spirit and His indwelling of us.

Each day we need to ask God to bring to our minds any sin we have in our lives, whether overt or intrinsic sins. These can be habits, attitudes, words or actions that inhibit us from being fruitful. We need to ask Christ to cover these sins with His blood and wash them out of us (sending them down the proverbial drain). Then, we need to ask God to fill us to overflowing with the Holy Spirit and the fruit He exhibits.

The gunk-filled sin in our lives tends to stick much easier than fruit. That's why it takes a daily renewal on our part of asking forgiveness of sins and indwelling of the Holy Spirit, from the top of our heads to the tip of our toes.This prayerful process will not only change our lives, but will change our day as well. Ridding our lives of the mud and gunk in our hearts is not only life changing to us, but to the people around us as well. Getting a good 'washing' on a daily basis is maintenance we all need.

May the Lord fill you to overflowing with love, joy, peace, patience, kindness, goodness, faithfulness, gentleness and self control.

In that, may the world know that Jesus loves us so!!

Seeds of Encouragement

Everyone around us benefits when we express the fruit of the Holy Spirit. Daily emptying ourselves of the mud and gunk in our lives will positively impact our day and ultimately affect those in our sphere of influence.

"The state of your life is nothing more than a reflection of your state of mind."

Wayne Dyer

FEAR NOT

"But now, this is what the LORD says - he who created you, O Jacob, he who formed you, O Israel: 'Fear not, for I have redeemed you; I have summoned you by name; you are mine. When you pass through the waters, I will be with you; and when you pass through the rivers, they will not sweep over you. When you walk through the fire, you will not be burned; the flames will not set you ablaze. For I am the LORD, your God, the Holy One of Israel, your Savior.'" (Isaiah 43:1-3)

It was past business hours and the simmering desert sun was just beginning to hide itself behind the mountains. My husband Matt and I were wheeling and dealing to purchase a car I had coveted for two years. It would be the perfect car for our expanding family and my expanding waistline. I was four months pregnant with our first son and everything in our world was good.

There was another family seated at a desk inside the dealership. They had three children who were approximately 7, 2 and 1. I was easily distracted by the children. I loved watching them take turns pushing the baby girl in the stroller. I could hardly wait until I would push my own son around and hear him giggle with delight as we danced with the stroller.

The salesperson was growing weary of our persistence on the price we were willing to pay. We were fatigued too, but I wanted that car. The other family finally left and we were alone in the large showroom. Our salesman came to again offer us his "bottom line pricing" and this time he had our attention with the numbers he presented. I looked at Matt, for a visual cue of yes or no. Before he could respond I heard a loud boom, tires screeching and glass breaking. I looked straight ahead and to my shock and disbelief there was a car airborne and flying straight towards us. I knew my life was over. I ducked my head and waited for impact.

The driver had his foot all the way down on the accelerator and the car flew through the 18 foot plate glass showroom window. Shards and chunks of glass flew everywhere. I felt the heat of the motor and heard the spinning of the tires as they flew past me. Blistering hot fluid and glass covered me, and then there was deafening silence. I looked to my right where my 16 year old niece Rachel had been seated. She and her chair were gone. Matt made sure I was alright and went to find Rachel. He found her under the car that had come to a stop against the opposite wall. She escaped the wreckage with battery acid burns to her back and leg.

I stood in shock at the sight and collapsed on the floor at the power of the scene, something straight out of an Arnold Schwarzenegger movie. This drunk driver was exceeding 80 miles per hour upon impact. The driver's girlfriend was in the car with him and she was also four months pregnant. Her baby did not survive. He also destroyed 3 brand new vehicles, including a convertible Mustang a proud owner had just driven off the car lot, as well as a street median and a stoplight. I escaped with a small gash on my shoulder. Matt was unharmed.

The definition of fear is "an emotion or alarm caused by danger". That day my life was forever changed and a paralyzing fear took root that crippled my existence. I was scared when Matt would leave the house, afraid that something horrible would happen.

I couldn't leave our home without first making sure everything was in order (just in case I didn't come back). Every decision, every act started with the uncertain question of "what if." I wouldn't drive out of town or leave my family for more than short periods of time. My fear held me captive and I carried the constant weight of the proverbial ball and chain. I begged God, "Release me from this stronghold!"

Three years later I had a dream. In my dream I was standing out in space and looking at the earth against the black backdrop of the universe. Jesus stood beside me. Without a word, one single white line began to circle the earth, again and again. It went on top of and underneath, intersecting this way and that like a ball of yarn. The line covered the earth until I could hardly see it anymore. Jesus then said to me, "Andrea, EVERY circumstance, EVERY situation in your life, your painful past, your worries of the present; EVERY day, in EVERY way is working for my glory." For a moment in time I experienced what I know I will experience in heaven; a peace that surpasses ALL comprehension.

My delivery from those chains did not happen immediately. But I have held on for dear life to those words Jesus gave me that night! I continued to pray, read God's Word and claim the promises He made for those who call him Abba, which translated in English means "daddy;" a daddy who is a complete gentleman, who loves and cares deeply for His children. One you can trust completely and who will hold you gently in His loving, protective arms forever.

In 2008, fear was headline news: gas prices, home foreclosures, job losses, wars and rumors of wars, to name a few. But our strength, our hope, our very foundation is found in nothing less than our faithful, loving Lord God Almighty, who was, and is and is to come. (Revelation 4:8)

You can trust Him. Psalm 27:1 says, "The LORD is my light and my salvation - whom shall I fear? The LORD is the stronghold of my life - of whom shall I be afraid?" Psalm 34:4 states: "I sought the LORD, and he answered me; he delivered me from all my fears."

Seeds of Encouragement

We all have fears, situations or circumstances in our lives that stop us in our tracks. But the great gift we've all been given is the opportunity to fall at the feet of the Savior who wants to abolish the chains which bind us. Jesus wants us to freely "run with perseverance the race marked out for us." (Hebrews 12:1)

So, beloved, keep looking to heaven. Keep your eyes on the ONLY non-changing aspect of this ever changing world, Jesus. "Say to those with fearful hearts, 'Be strong, do not fear; your God will come, he will come with vengeance; with divine retribution he will come to save you.'" (Isaiah 35:4) Isaiah 41:10 promises, "So do not fear, for I am with you; do not be dismayed, for I am your God. I will strengthen you and help you; I will uphold you with my righteous right hand."

Hold on and don't let go, dear child. He has you in His grasp. Let go of fear and let Him hold you.

Seeds of Encouragement

We all have fears in our lives that can lead us into bondage. God calls us to lay those chains at His feet on a daily basis and live the abundant life He has for each of us.

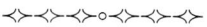

"God is our refuge and strength, a very present help in trouble."
Psalm 46:1

Hopping Hurdles

Growing up I was very much a tomboy. Living in Oklahoma we were nuts about sports. Tackle football was my passion and I was in the middle of any game I could find. I loved dragging my opponent to the ground. No matter how big or small, they did not intimidate me. My dream was to play professional football for the Pittsburgh Steelers.

Aside from football, I enjoyed most active sports. Living in a small town I was able to participate in everything our school offered. I could run pretty fast, so in track I ran sprints and relays each year. It's what I knew. That is, until Coach Graham arrived.

He was tall and athletic with an infectious smile that caught everyone's attention. He had a hearty belief in bringing out the best in his students. Refusal to give your all was not something he let us get away with. He was convinced I should and could jump hurdles. I was the lofty height of 5'2"! How was I going to run hurdles?

Being new to our community he simply didn't understand that I did sprints, NOT hurdles. I would explain that to him and everything would be fine. Our conversation did not go as I anticipated. He said, "Great! You can run sprints AND hurdles." He thought I could do it and we were going to work on those hurdles every day until I mastered them. Failure was not an option.

Day after day I ran the hurdles, jumping over them while my legs burned from fatigue. As soon as I finished a timed trial, I was able to rest for a minute. Then Coach Graham would chuckle and say, "All right, let's do it again." My body never hurt so much. My legs felt like jello and cried out for me to stop. The air was humid and hot and I hated the hurdles with every breath. But Coach Graham's confidence never wavered. He believed that I could not only participate, but win. He firmly believed practice makes perfect.

The county track meet arrived and I lined up in my lane. The spikes on my shoes dug into the red clay track. The gun went off and I ran like crazy, jumping each hurdle. I counted my steps in between hurdles and miraculously glided over each one. To my complete astonishment I crossed the finish line in first place. I could not believe it! What a thrill! I was eligible for the finals.

The time came for the final. My heart was pounding. I bolted from the starting block and was in the lead. On the last hurdle I hit it with my back foot and fell on the track. I jumped to my feet and dashed for the finish line. I came in third. I was out of breath and disgruntled. Blood from the fall oozed down my leg, The announcement came over the loud speaker that the first and second place girls were going to compete at the state competition. Coach Graham put his arm around me, smiled and said, "We'll get them next year."

Over the years, I have often thought back to the lessons I learned through that rigorous training. Sometimes life is hard. We strive, struggle and sweat to get over numerous hurdles. Relationships, finances, careers, kids and health are just a few.

Each one of us has issues or hurdles that we are trying to hop over. But through it all God is ever-present. He loves and adores each one of His children. He deeply desires to have a personal relationship with every one of us.

The Bible is as relevant today as it was 2,000 years ago. Times have changed but people have not. His Word is full of promises for you and me to claim each time we run in this race called life. Romans 8:31 says, "What, then, shall we say in response to this? If God is for us, who can be against us?" Philippians 4:13 states, "I can do everything through him who gives me strength." And, as the young teenager David stood in defiance against the giant Goliath, he knew that God was able to help him in conquering his foe.

When Joshua was preparing to lead the Israelites into the Promised Land, God reminded Joshua that He would never leave or forsake him. God went on to say in Joshua 1:9, "Have I not commanded you? Be strong and courageous. Do not be terrified; do not be discouraged, for the LORD your God will be with you WHEREVER you go." (emphasis mine) What a promise! God cannot lie. If He says it, you can believe it!

When I was running the hurdle races, I could only jump over one hurdle at a time. With each one I approached I had to be prepared. My stride and stance had to be correct. That's why day to day training was so very important.

So it is in our life training as well. In order to be prepared, we must discipline ourselves into a daily habit of Bible study and prayer. Our lives will simply not be as strong without it. I tell our boys there's no power without prayer, and Bible reading too. In order to be strong and courageous we must have a daily diet of those two.

Be encouraged dear one! Take one hurdle at a time and face it head on with prayer and God's Word. Our victory is at hand!

Seeds of Encouragement

Each one of us has hurdles in life we're trying to hop over. With a daily regimen of Bible reading and prayer we'll find the moment by moment strength we need to finish victoriously.

"Perfection is not attainable,
but if we chase perfection we can catch excellence."

Vince Lombardi

God is Without Limits

Struggling to make ends meet, a young, single mom wonders just how she and her precious daughter will make it. The heavy fog that encases the neighborhood matches her mood perfectly. Dreary, depressing and with no sun in sight Janice (not her real name) cries out to God for help and assurance.

As a single mom, Janice often worried if she was meeting all the needs of her daughter, Brittani (not her real name). Janice often felt inept and unqualified for the daunting task God had blessed her with in raising a daughter. Insecurities flooded her heart. This gift of motherhood was unlike any treasure she possessed. Brittani was her life and she dedicated all she had to her. Janice wanted so badly to be a good mom, but she often found herself questioning her abilities.

She was thankful for the meager paying job she had, but also frustrated because this was not the position she had been educated for. Filling out applications and going to countless interviews for over a year have led nowhere. Christmas was fast approaching. "Lord, what will I do? I have nothing to give Brittani. Please show me the way and help us through", she prayed.

One day a woman walked into Janice's workplace. The woman was well dressed and had a cheerful attitude. She smiled frequently and was very polite. She ordered the materials she needed and paid Janice for her supplies. Expressing thanks for Janice's service, she walked out the door.

A few minutes later the cheerful customer reappeared. Janice thought maybe she'd made a mistake with her order. The woman simply smiled at Janice and said, "God's told me I need to tell you some things." Janice stared wide eyed at the woman. Was she for real, she wondered?

The woman began, "God wants you to know you're a good mother. Although you question yourself, God doesn't. He knows you've doubted yourself and He knows you worry about meeting your daughter's needs. God is proud of you and appreciates your heart in being all you can for her. He knows you're struggling financially. God wants you to know things will get easier very soon. Your needs will be met." By this time Janice's eyes were filled with tears. This woman she'd never met was telling her the very burdens Janice had in her heart. With awe and wonder, Janice thanked the woman, who was soon on her way.

Within the next two weeks the county position that Janice had been trying to obtain for over a year called and offered her a full time position. To this day, Janice has never seen the woman again. She often wonders if this was an angel sent by God or a modern day prophet obeying God's heed to speak as she was told.

The Bible says in Isaiah 55:8 "'For my thoughts are not your thoughts, neither are your ways my ways,' declares the LORD." God is not limited by time, people, places, events or hearts. He IS, and always has been. He knows what has been and what will be. He is all knowing, all loving and cares deeply for the heart concerns of every one of his children, whether or not they acknowledge Him. God is without limits.

Whatever you are facing today, your heart cries are being heard. "Trust in the Lord with all your heart and do not lean on your own understanding. In all your ways acknowledge Him and He will direct your paths." Proverbs 3:5-6 NIV.

Happy Mother's Day to every precious mom!

Seeds of Encouragement

God is not limited by time, people, places, events or hearts.
He IS, and always will be. He is all knowing, all loving and cares
deeply for the concerns of every one of His children.
God is without limits!

In this Desert Place

Why am I here, how did I come?
I desire an oasis of
shade, shelter, rest, and time;

But find tears, waiting, pleading,
parched, spent
prayer, and pondering.

I walk, seek and wait.
Only to find there's more time,
More steps to take.

Consider this: My grace is sufficient
even in this desert place.

My presence is constant,
even in this desert place.

My love never changes,
even in this desert place.

Lessons gleaned are not instant.
Refinement requires heat, pounding and cold.

But when our time is over,
We'll have gained wisdom, compassion and fortitude
that others will find solace in.

Our lives our not our own, and for those
who travel in the desert place,
we will never be the same.

Andrea Sharp

Attitude

"I discovered I always have choices and sometimes it's only a choice of attitude"

Judith M. Knowlton

Seeds of Encouragement

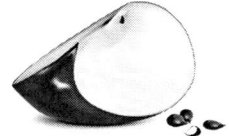

Attitude; everyone has one. In the blink of an eye, our attitude can lift a person's heart to soar or plunge them to a miry pit. We cannot choose what each day entails, but we can choose the attitude in which we respond. How I desire to choose an attitude that brings life to the moment. I know I fail often, but it's an aspiration worth pursuing. Be encouraged today as you seek to influence your sphere with an attitude that wows!

Whatever!

In the hustle and bustle of everyday life,

With an abundance of stress

And an abundance of strife!

Whatever my day, whatever my 'tude',

God desires me to bless with my mood.

Jesus came to bring me life more abundantly

To give me hope and love, eternally.

My heart's cry is to bring glory to God,

In all that I do and wherever I trod.

So whatever my day and whatever my 'tude',

Jesus is my source of strength and delight

In all that I do!

Andrea Sharp

Pish, Posh

We were in a mad dash to get in the car. We were running behind, so I grabbed the car keys and jumped in the car. My oldest son Clay wiggled between the small space of the car and garage wall to get in as well. As he opened the door, he growled, "Oh, GROSS! This is disgusting!" Thinking he was being overly dramatic at the state of our garage floor, I quickly dismissed his comment, and said, "Get in! We're leaving!" "Mom," he exclaimed, "Jojo ate a bird!" Wonderful, I sighed. Jojo is our family cat. He's a very large, dominating, black and white cat. As far as cats go, he rules our neighborhood.

When we arrived back at home I grudgingly entered our dead bird domain and vacuumed up the plethora of feathers. Earlier in the week I had seen a neighbor's cat in our back yard sneaking up on an unsuspecting bird; or so it seemed. The cat would slowly creep closer to the group of birds having breakfast. The birds continued pecking and eating. All of a sudden the cat pounced, but missed the mark. The birds took flight and were gone in an instant.

Apparently, one bird was not fast enough to escape Jojo's grasp, because I was now cleaning up the remnants of his prize.

I thought of my own life and how many times I have acted like those birds. Playing with temptation and praying not to get eaten. Because I don't want my boys to make the same stupid mistakes I have made in life, I often tell them that when they are tempted, to run like a deer away from what is tempting them. Not saunter, but dash away!

I feel like I didn't get a brain until I was about 37 years old. My boys are much faster learners than I was, so my hopes are high that they won't follow in my own foolish footsteps.

Seeds of Encouragement

What temptations or struggles do you face today? I know (because I was one of them) that many think they can play with fire and not get burned. We have a "pish, posh" attitude. So what, no one will know. Oh, beloved, that simply is not true. Sexual promiscuity, experimenting with alcohol and drugs, lying, shoplifting or trying to cheat in school, work or taxes all lead to disaster.

We're tempted to think we won't get caught. That is a lie from the pit of hell! Galatians 6:7 states "Do not be deceived. God is not mocked. A man reaps what he sows." The great news is we have an awesome accountability partner in Jesus. He sees and knows all. There is nothing hidden from Him and all is laid bare in His sight. Anything done in the dark WILL be exposed in the light.

1 Peter 5:8-9 says, "Be sober and self controlled. Be watchful. Your adversary, the devil walks around like a roaring lion, seeking whom he may devour." God knows what we our temptation is.. Hebrews 2:18 says, "Because he himself has suffered when he was tempted, he is able to help those who are being tempted."

Praise God we're not alone in our fight for doing right, but Christ, our Redeemer, Savior and friend is always willing to come to our aid. All we have to do is ask and He runs to our side, ready to do battle in our place.

We can also take some positive steps to combat temptation. Read the Bible each day. It's filled with victorious stories of those who have faced struggles. It's packed with God-breathed words to encourage and strengthen us. Spend time in prayer. Sitting at the feet of Jesus will drastically change our lives. Also, get an accountability partner, someone who you can call in time of need; they in turn will touch base with you regularly to see how things are going and pray for you. Another great resource we have is Christian music which keeps us centered on what is holy and true.

My favorite way to stay tuned into God is to turn off the TV. It's not called the 'boob tube' by accident. There's rarely anything on that encourages us to love God more. The 'off' button is a powerful tool! I encourage you to become very familiar with it.

"With God on our side, who can be against us?" Paul exclaims in the book of Romans. Dear ones, it's time for us to take up our armor and do battle the right way, with God as our focus and righteousness as our goal. The victory is ours!

Seeds of Encouragement

What temptations do you face today? What are you struggling with? Praise God we're not alone in our fight for doing right, but Christ, our Redeemer, Savior and friend is always willing to come to our aid. All we have to do is ask and He runs to our side, ready to do battle in our place. What a friend we have in Jesus!

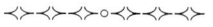

"I never expect to lose. Even when I'm the underdog, I still prepare a victory speech."

H. Jackson Brown, Jr.

A Matter of Perspective

My boys have been raised in the era of toys that make noise. A trip to the store exposes them to an array of items with the words, "push me or try me." Once the button is pushed children squeal with delight as the contraption begins wiggling and blaring some annoying sound that only a child would appreciate. Every parent knows this and tries desperately to stay away from such areas in the stores. This was my desire as well, but this particular day, well....you'll see.

We were in a rush. We needed a birthday gift fast and time was short. The party would be starting soon! In the Target parking lot I grabbed my youngest son Landon's little hand and we dashed into the store. It was filled with hanging paraphernalia which instantly caught the attention of Landon. "Mom, look at that!" he cried, "do you see the Spider Man picture?" "Uh, huh," I mumbled. I was on a mission and nothing was going to distract me.

"Landon, hurry honey," I pleaded, "We're going to be late." "But my foot hurts, Mom." Landon said. "Why does it hurt?" I asked. Clearly I was trying to sympathize. "I don't know," he said. Still holding his hand and rushing through the aisles, Landon pleaded, "Mom, it still hurts." I sighed, "Ok, let's see what's wrong."

We stopped in one of the middle aisles and I stooped down to untie his dirty shoestrings, straighten them, adjust the shoe tongue and retie. As I was working on the second shoe, intent on fixing the hurt, Landon said, "Mom, it's not working." "Mmm," I replied, my head down, still working on his shoe. "Mom, these don't work," he repeated. "Ah, ha!" I exclaimed. Those shoes would no longer bring discomfort! "Look, Mom, these don't work," Landon repeated. "What doesn't work, honey?" My frustration was beginning to surface.

He sighed heavily. "These!!" he said, clearly irritated. I looked up. Lo and behold, we were standing amidst the lingerie section. He was reading a sign over some bras that said, "Push up." He kept pushing but NOTHING was happening! No bells, music or movement of any kind. They simply hung there. Not wanting to get into a woman's physique discussion with a 7 year old, I just said, "Huh, I wonder why?" Then, clutching his tiny hand, we were off on our mission again.

What's your perspective this Easter season? Is it a time just for pretty dresses, Easter egg hunting and Easter dinner with family? Or is it a celebration of what Jesus Christ did for us on the cross? He gave all He could give, so we could experience abundant life and live forever in His presence. He absolutely adores you, beloved! John 3:16 says, "For God SO LOVED the world, that He gave His one and only Son, that WHOEVER believes in Him shall not perish but have eternal life." (Emphasis mine)

Happy Holy season! Let's keep our perspective on what's true and remember to stay away from the lingerie aisles!

Seeds of Encouragement
Sometimes our perspectives get tainted and skewed.
When that happens we have an advocate to help us gain a clearer picture of reality.
Look to God; ask for wisdom and clarity.
Beloved, He will give it to you!

Connecting

"Do not forget to entertain strangers, for by so doing some people have entertained angels without knowing it."

Hebrews 13:2

Seeds of Encouragement

"Though one may be overpowered, two can defend themselves. A cord of three strands is not quickly broken."

Ecclesiastes 4:12

Angels Unaware

"For he will command his angels concerning you to guard you in all your ways; they will lift you up in their hands." Psalm 91:11-12

I rushed to the hospital soon after my husband had taken his mom to the emergency room because she was having trouble breathing. Mom going to the ER was not something new. In the past year she had been admitted two other times. Being 89, having dementia and Parkinson's disease she sometimes needed the extra care that hospitals provide. As soon as I entered her room, I knew her condition was dire. She was lying on the bed unable to speak and there was a tremendous gurgling noise with every breath. I leaned over her, kissed her and whispered, "Hi Mom. I love you! You're going to be ok." She tried to speak, but couldn't and fear filled her eyes. I gently rubbed her arm and repeated "It's ok, Mom." I turned to my husband, Matt and said, "You better call your family. They need to get here." Matt looked at my quizzically, but when my expression didn't falter, he knew I was serious.

Tests showed Mom had double pneumonia and had suffered a heart attack. Once the nurses got her settled into her room, they administered oxygen, took her vitals and asked to speak with us in the hall. After a doctor's review the nurse sweetly told us they would do everything they could to keep her comfortable and that if we needed anything at all to please let them know. Matt and I stood silently, unsure of what to do. Finally, he said, "What does that mean?" I looked into those sweet eyes and said, "Honey, they mean she's terminal and this is it." He looked away and breathed a deep, heavy sigh. The youngest of four children, Matt was always the one whom his parents could count on to take care of things. This time was no different. Matt quickly switched into 'go mode' (as he calls it) and went to tell his dad the bad news.

Seeds of Encouragement

Hours passed and people came in and out. Family soon began arriving and Mom was still conscious, but unable to speak. Her husband of 70 years hovered over her with kisses and "I love you"s. We read to Mom, sang to her, and prayed over her. The nurses told us that the last sense to go is the hearing. It was a comfort to us that hopefully she could at least hear her family talk to her.

The hospital staff was incredibly gracious and sympathetic. They attentively cared for Mom's needs and ours too. They brought in a tray of bottled water, coffee and cookies. They did all they could do, answering our many questions, bringing in extra chairs and setting up a guest bed for us to stay the night.

Three days later Mom passed away at home with Matt, our boys and me by her side. We kissed her soft cheeks, caressed her hands and told her how much we loved her. She left this world being loved and entered into the arms of the One who has always adored and loved her completely.

The next week was a blur. Matt finalized the funeral arrangements and the day arrived for us to take my father-in-law (Dad) to Fresno for Mom's service at their home church. The day was beautiful! My own family came and surrounded us with such love and care. Dad got to see family and friends he hadn't seen in a long time. We ate lunch and Dad thanked the many loved ones who had come.

We headed home after a very tiring day. We were almost to Kingsburg when I turned to see Dad unresponsive in the seat behind me. He had vomited and was unconscious. Matt pulled the car off the freeway and we jumped into the back seat. Dad wasn't responding to us and began gasping for air.

We knew we had to get some help. Matt gunned the accelerator and we exited off the freeway. There was a McDonald's there, so we pulled into the parking lot. I ran inside to get some wet paper towels. Dad came to a little and Matt helped him out of the car. He vomited again and fainted, collapsing in our arms. All the while, our three precious boys were watching every move from the car window. "What's wrong with him, Mom?" "Is he dying?" Answers escaped us. We simply didn't have any.

Almost immediately, a man and two women ran up to help us. The man was an EMT with the local fire department and one of the women was a nurse. They began taking his vitals and calling 911. The other woman was a teacher. She started talking to our boys, asking their ages and what school they went to. Her friendly smile and demeanor put our boys at ease and they were soon chatting away. The fire department, police personnel and an ambulance quickly arrived. The nurse and EMT gave the specifics to them. The teacher asked if she could take our boys into McDonald's and get them something to eat. We both numbly nodded ok.

At the emergency room, after numerous tests it was determined that Dad was overly emotional and exhausted from the past week. He spent a couple of days resting in the hospital.

Psalm 34:7 says, "The angel of the LORD encamps around those who fear him, and he delivers them." And Isaiah says, "Do you not know? Have you not heard? The LORD is the everlasting God, the Creator of the ends of the earth. He will not grow tired or weary, and his understanding no one can fathom. He gives strength to the weary and increases the power of the weak. Even youths grow tired and weary, and young men stumble and fall; but those who hope in the LORD will renew their strength. They will soar on wings like eagles; they will run and not grow weary, they will walk and not be faint." Isaiah 40:28-31

Seeds of Encouragement

Looking back to this time of Mom and Dad's hospitalizations, Matt and I have no doubt we were ministered to by the very hands of God. Jesus said in Matthew 25:40, "I tell you the truth, whatever you did for one of the least of these brothers of mine, you did for me." People who delivered meals, those who cried and prayed with us, family members, emergency and hospital staff were all ministers of grace in our time of need.

Isn't it incredible that God sends people to us at just the right time to strengthen and uphold us? These 'angels unaware' do what they can to love and help. Whether they realize it or not, when they help those in need, they are being the hands and feet of Christ. Galatians 6:9-10 states, "Let us not become weary in doing good, for at the proper time we will reap a harvest if we do not give up. Therefore, as we have opportunity, let us do well to all people, especially to those who belong to the family of believers." With every act of kindness, various people in their differing roles blessed and encouraged us in a dark hour.

Who can you minister to today? Who can you help uphold? A neighbor in need, a co-worker who's brokenhearted, or a friend who's at the end of their rope? All around us are opportunities for doing good; for showing a needy world that God loves and adores them. Provide a meal, visit a shut in, do yard work for an elderly couple, invite a family over for dinner, call to encourage and pray with someone, or simply let someone know you care.

It's been said that at the worst of times, people are at their best. I am a believer of that! In these uncertain times, may we all be gracious and giving to those in need. In so doing, may the whole world know that Jesus loves you so!

Seeds of Encouragement

Isn't it incredible how God sends people to us at just the right moment to strengthen and uphold us? These 'angels unaware' minister grace and love in our time of need, and in so doing reflect the hands and feet of Christ.

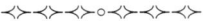

"They may forget what you said but they will never forget how you made them feel."

Carol Buchner

What a Difference a Teacher Makes

"And whoever welcomes a little child like this in my name welcomes me." Matthew 18:5

It was a cold and cloudy day. Rain threatened to fall. The weather matched our moods. The somber graveside service was in honor of a young husband and father. His beautiful wife sat silently beside her two children. She looked up and gestured to friends. They came and stood beside her to lend their support. As I watched, they gently smiled at the grieving widow.

As I stood there silently, I began to ponder the incredible impact these people, the children's teachers, had on this family. The teachers had been pivotal in the family's lives for over two years. They had lovingly supported the family as the once vibrant husband and father contracted an unknown illness and never returned home from the hospital. What a difference a teacher makes.

During my elementary school days my teachers left a lasting impression on me. The extreme weather in Oklahoma played havoc with Mom's asthma and she was hospitalized often. When she was in the hospital, she entrusted me to those whom she knew would care for me both inside and out of the classroom: teachers.

My second grade teacher was Miss Cook. She was just another teacher to me until my mom had to go into the hospital and I needed to stay Miss Cook. Sensing my reluctance in being there, she quickly won my favor by making my favorite meal – macaroni and cheese. We topped off the evening by making gingerbread cookies. From that day forward, I had a new attitude toward her. She gave of herself for my benefit and I never forgot it.

Seeds of Encouragement

In third grade I stayed with my teacher Mrs. Schnaithman for a number of days. Each morning on the way to school, Mrs. Schnaithman would quiz me on my multiplication tables. Over and over we would review them. I learned those multiplication tables perfectly! In fourth grade I stayed with my teacher Mrs. Stehno. She introduced me to cow's tongue stew. Yes, they really do make this and people eat it too! When I balked at the thought of having it for dinner she just laughed and said, "Well, if you're hungry enough you'll eat." I sometimes hear myself say these same words to my own boys.

In fifth and sixth grade, I stayed with Mrs. McClusky. She had two daughters who were in college. Their bedrooms were very 'girly girl'. It was so much fun to lie on their beds and look at their pretty decor. I dreamed of someday having a room that looked like theirs. These teachers sacrificially gave of themselves and their time. What a difference a teacher makes.

Those of us who have contact with children have to be lovingly intentional in our times with them. Our interaction and words will have a lasting impact. My oldest son gets frustrated when I can't remember which basketball team he played last week, but I remember the names of teachers I had years ago. I bet you can also remember special teacher's names.

Hanging on my refrigerator for what seems like forever is a piece of paper I scribbled some words on reminding me to be intentional with my children. It says, "Love them, laugh with them, play with them and pray with them – EVERYDAY!" There are some days in which I fail miserably at this, but nevertheless, it's my goal each day. Matthew 18:6 warns us to deal gently with little ones. It states, "But if anyone causes one of these little ones who believe in me to sin, it would be better for him to have a large millstone hung around his neck and to be drowned in the depths of the sea."

Seeds of Encouragement

Beloved, for those of us who have the incredible blessing of interacting with children we have a responsibility to be positive role models. The Lord just loves it when we nurture and guide them according to His way. Jesus didn't merely tell people how to behave, He always set an example. I know Jesus had an incredible impact on the children He was around. I can just picture children running around the Lord, pulling on His robe, wanting to share their many tales with Him. God is the ultimate good listener and I know His sweet Son was the same way during His time on earth. He has a special soft spot in His heart for little ones, and so must we.

May we be lovingly intentional in our actions and words with God's children. In this, may they know that Jesus loves them so.

Forest E. Witcraft wrote, "One hundred years from now, it will not matter what my bank account was, how big my house was, or what kind of car I drove. But the world may be a little better, because I was important in the life of a child." What a difference a teacher makes.

Seeds of Encouragement

Those of us who have the incredible blessing of interacting with children have a responsibility to be positive role models.
We never know how our influence will help determine their steps down the road.

Parenting

"Before I got married I had six theories about bringing up children; now I have six children, and no theories."

John Wilmot

"Any fool can be a Father, but it takes a real man to be a Daddy!!"

Philip Whitmore

Seeds of Encouragement

As parents we sometimes don't feel like we're having an impact in our children's lives. Activities, friends and media all consume so much of kids' time and attention. But our impact is real. The way we live day to day is a silent example on how life should be lived. We are influencing our children. The question is, are we influencing them positively or negatively? We have a choice in the legacy we're living and ultimately leaving.

Daddy Dearest

"I'm not a father... am I?" The words came slowly out of my husband Matt's mouth and he stood with a confused look on his face. I had proudly handed Matt his very first Father's Day card. He had just walked into my parent's house after driving up from southern California, where we lived at the time. We were visiting them for Memorial Day weekend. I was so giddy I could hardly stand it!

I had taken a pregnancy test earlier in the day in the restroom of a local Mexican restaurant. My stunned mom couldn't stand to wait the three minutes it took to get the results and began knocking on the door. "Look, Mom, it's negative," I sighed. "Let's look," Mom replied. "Andrea!" she screamed, "It's showing two lines - it's POSITIVE!" My jaw dropped - I couldn't believe it! "I'm going to be a mom!" We embraced in the cramped bathroom and went to tell my dad, who was waiting with the food that had arrived at our table.

I couldn't eat. My stomach fluttered with excitement! "Let's stop at the store and get Matt a Father's Day card." I said to my parents. My thrilled mom smiled. "Alright, let's go." To which my dad replied, "Wait, we just got our food." "Pack it up!" Mom said, "We're going to buy a card for Matt."

The truth was it was quite a shock for all of us. Matt and I had been married for six years. My mom still proudly carried a picture of our beautiful "little girl" Onyx, in her wallet. She was a purebred German Shepherd and she had all the rights and privileges of a family member. We'd always planned to have children. But three years turned to five years, and so on. Now it was official. We were going to be parents!

Seeds of Encouragement

Our son Clay was born eight months later and that day changed our lives forever. It was no longer about us or our wants, but about Clay and his needs. When he whimpered, we jumped. Each day we fell more and more in love with him and our parenthood role. Three years later brought our second son, Jaden. As his arrival day neared, embarrassed at the thought, I whispered to Matt one night as we lay in bed. "What if I don't love our Jaden as much as I do Clay?" "Honey, you will, you'll see," Matt reassuringly said. Jaden arrived and as he lay sleeping on my chest that first night together, my love for him was so deep I cried as I held him.

A year and a half later we lost a baby because of an ectopic pregnancy. Shattered by the loss, I begged God for another child. One day after 9/11, I found out I was pregnant. As our family mourned the loss of our baby, and the nation mourned the loss of its innocence, new life was beginning. Months passed and we were blessed with our son Landon. My mourning turned to joy.

Having children has given us the rare opportunity to catch a glimpse of how our heavenly Father loves us. There's nothing Matt and I wouldn't do to protect or provide for our boys. We rejoice over successes and hurt when they experience pain or sadness. There's nothing they can do or say that will change our love for them.

Jesus referred to His Father as 'Abba', which expresses a deep affection and is closely related to our term 'daddy.' Romans 8:39 says nothing "can separate us from the love of God that is in Christ Jesus our Lord." Nothing! Nada! In this we can put our whole trust and foundation.

As a daddy Matt is keenly aware that his role as our boys' earthly father is to model our heavenly Father and if he forgets this fact I'm quick to remind him. Our desire is that our boys would see God's reflection in us each day. Sometimes, we fail miserably. But God in His faithfulness leads us lovingly back to our task at hand, reminding us we have no greater assignment in this season.

Dads, be encouraged this day! Your role is pivotal in the heart of your children. When you are intentional about loving your kids, seeds of memories are stored in their minds. My dad took us camping, cliff diving, and canoeing down rivers. His efforts for quality time were often met with groans, complaints and arguments. But now that we're grown, we look back at those times as such fun and adventure! We're so thankful he took the time to make memories!

One of my favorite movies is Top Gun. The character Maverick is discouraged and thinking seriously about throwing in the towel and quitting his naval flight training at the vaunted Miramar Air Station. During a flying mission, he hesitates to engage the enemy and pulls back, not having the confidence to continue. His partner pleas with him, "Engage, engage, engage!"

So...Dad, it's your time to engage fully with your children. Give them the 'Triple T' they so desperately need: Time, tender touch and talk. What memories will you make together during this time? When you get discouraged, take a breath and remember you're not alone. All dads get discouraged. Few children are naturally appreciative. But the positive moments you're making DO MAKE A DIFFERENCE in their lives.

Engage with your kids dads! We're so very thankful for you! Happy Father's Day!

Seeds of Encouragement

Having children has given us the rare opportunity to catch a glimpse of how our heavenly Father loves us. We rejoice over successes, and hurt when they experience pain or sadness. There's nothing they can do or say that will change our love for them.

Parenting is the most important job we'll ever have! God gives us the blueprint of successful parenting in His Word, the Bible. The love He expresses to us is the same love we need to exhibit to our children. And with His help each day we CAN do it!

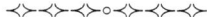

"I looked on childrearing not only as a work of love and duty but as a profession that was fully interesting and challenging as any honorable profession in the world and one that demanded the best that I could bring to it."

Rose Kennedy

What Can I Give Him

Oh, how I've longed for you and waited for this day,
I knelt before my awesome God each day, for you to pray.

I've dreamed of you and talked of you,
And wondered what you'd be.

I can't believe it's almost time for us to finally see,
The times we'd spend together laughing in the sun,

Your crawl, your first step, and then to watch you run.
What can I give you, you have most everything.

Daddy and I've made sure you're welcomed like a king.
What can I give you, my precious son?

I want it to be so special; for you are our very first one.
I asked the Lord and He replied in the kindest way,

"Dear child, look up and see the heavenly way.
The gift you can give does not come from earth,
It comes from Me and what I've taught since before your birth.
A legacy, a heritage of My unfailing love,
Forgiveness, salvation and faith from above.

It's not something he can hold that will become so dear,
But you teaching him, expressing love to which he'll cling so near.
To gaze his eyes on Me each day is the gift that he needs most,
Shepherding him and leading him, in that, girl you can boast!"

Andrea Sharp

Living a Legacy

"Tell me about heaven, Mommy," my seven year old son Landon said. For such a young one he is inquisitive about God and about what heaven will be like. My heart just melts that he loves to hear the things of God. Landon is our youngest son. He has blond hair, sparkling blue eyes and a face full of freckles. He often doesn't sleep well at night, but he quickly relaxes and settles down when we discuss what it will be like when he meets our sweet Jesus face to face.

Discussions of God and our relationship with Him are natural occurrences at our home and have been since our boys came out of the womb. Our biggest desire is to show our children who Jesus is, how much He cares and how He loves us.

It hasn't always been that way though. For the first few years of our marriage we were very 'me minded.' We both had head knowledge of the supremacy of God, but insignificant heart change. Once our first son was born, our whole outlook on life was suddenly and drastically altered. We wanted to 'live a legacy' in sharing Jesus.

A legacy is a gift by will (a bequest), or to hand down something of great value.

We wanted our son and future sons to grow up loving Jesus. We knew it was our job as their parents to train them in that. This process wasn't going to happen by simply sitting in a pew on Sunday mornings; we had to make life changes.

It was time for us to take seriously the roles we play in this life in reflecting the light and love of God. No more closet Christians for us; we were going to live our faith out loud. If we loved Jesus, then those around us should know it. "Only be careful, and watch yourselves closely so that you do not forget the things your eyes have seen or let them slip from your heart as long as you live. Teach them to your children and to their children after them." Deuteronomy 4:9

We are not perfect in our quest by any means. There have been many times we have missed the mark of the example we wanted to provide. In raising our boys, we want them to know AND live the fact that this life isn't all there is. We want them to be kingdom and eternally minded, realizing what they do or don't do in this life has everlasting implications.

Dear friends, this life we live is a speck of time. It's merely a grain of sand. When our lives are over, our time on earth will be a mere blip on the radar screen. Ecclesiastes 3:11 says, "He has made everything beautiful in its time. He has also set eternity in the hearts of men; yet they cannot fathom what God has done from beginning to end."

Beloved, when we die, our souls will live on eternally, either in heaven where we will forever be in the presence of God, or in hell forever separated from God. For some, this is hard to swallow, I realize, but it is no less true. 2 Timothy 4:3-4 states, "For the time will come when men will not put up with sound doctrine. Instead, to suit their own desires, they will gather around them a great number of teachers to say what their itching ears want to hear. They will turn their ears away from the truth and turn aside to myths."

Friends, I love you and care for you too much to 'tickle' your ears. Time is too short and we need to seize the day for God while we have the opportunity. Philippians 2:10-11 says, "That at the name of Jesus every knee should bow, in heaven and on earth and under the earth, and every tongue confess that Jesus Christ is Lord, to the glory of God the Father."

The day is coming, sweet friend. Our face to face appointment with God has been set in the eternal date book since the beginning of time. Are you ready?

This is the day to begin living a legacy; a legacy of loving Jesus with all your heart and soul. You will NEVER regret it! In this, may the whole world know that Jesus loves us so!

Seeds of Encouragement

This life we live is a speck of time. It's merely a grain of sand.
Let's not put off until tomorrow the good we can do today.

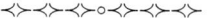

"Feelings of worth can flourish only in an atmosphere where individual differences are appreciated, mistakes are tolerated, communication is open, and rules are flexible -- the kind of atmosphere that is found in a nurturing family."

Virginia Satir

Raising 'G Rated' Kids in an 'R Rated' World

"Choose for yourselves this day whom you will serve...But as for me and my household, we will serve the LORD." Joshua 24:15

Recently, I was on the coast teaching at a women's conference on the subject of raising G rated kids in an R rated world. The topic is an eye opener as it's not something that is easily attained in our modern culture. Parents are longing for ways to tame the rising tide of influence on their young.

Being a mom myself to three bustling, growing boys, I have heard the argument many times from those who say to my husband Matt and I, "Kids have to experience 'the real world' sooner or later. Sheltering them from what's out there is just setting them up for failure. When they get out in the 'real world' they simply won't know what to do." To that I simply say, "Hogwash!" How wise would it be for me to ask my six year old to drive my car around the block, just to get used to the feel and handle of it? For certainly, someday he will be driving; and sheltering him from the real world experience now will only inhibit and harm him in his future driving experiences. What parent wouldn't think I was completely off my rocker if I did that?? I would be fined and possibly jailed for my neglect (and rightfully so!)

Why then, do we think that it's ok for our kids to experience other scenarios before they are mature and old enough to handle them? Inappropriate movies, TV, video games, books/magazines, music and computer sites have a HUGE impact on our children and their hearts, from which all actions and attitudes derive.

I speak with parents all the time who are frustrated over the impact these things have on their children. The world says it's no big deal. But God has something very different to say.

Seeds of Encouragement

In Deuteronomy 6:5-9 it says, "Love the LORD your God with all your heart and with all your soul and with all your strength. These commandments that I give you today are to be upon your hearts. Impress them on your children. Talk about them when you sit at home and when you walk along the road, when you lie down and when you get up. Tie them as symbols on your hands and bind them on your foreheads. Write them on the doorframes of your houses and on your gates." Verse 12 goes on to say, "…Be careful that you do not forget the LORD…" (Emphasis mine)

Beloved, it's time for us to get serious about where and on what our kids are spending the majority of their time. IT WILL AND DOES HAVE AN INFLUENCE, for good or for bad!!

When I was a little girl, we would decorate and hide Easter eggs; yes the real kind, not plastic. In the extreme Oklahoma weather, sometimes we were unable to hide our eggs outside. We would take turns hiding the eggs around the house and finding them. But invariably, we would come up short in our efforts in locating all of them. We would rack our brains trying to figure out where we had put them, but there was always a stray egg we couldn't account for.

Days later the familiar pungent smell would begin to linger throughout our home. Room by room we would search to see where the smell was most present. Usually we would find the rotting egg in some dark corner, a closet or behind an appliance in the kitchen. It was very difficult getting rid of the disgusting smell, but slowly the fumes would dissipate and our home would be back to normal.

Our hearts are like that. What we view, listen to and invest in will permeate our thoughts, attitudes and actions. Our children are no different. Philippians 4:8 says, "Finally, brothers, whatever is true, whatever is noble, whatever is right, whatever is pure, whatever is lovely, whatever is admirable- if ANYTHING is excellent or praiseworthy-think about such things. (Emphasis mine)

God desires that EVERY corner of our hearts and minds belong to Him. Children are especially vulnerable to the lies of our culture. Lies such as, showing more is better and wearing clothes with designs or words that bring attention to private body areas makes them cool and more desirable. What parent wants anyone looking at their child's butt or cleavage?

But know this: when our girls wear shorts or pants that have words on the bottom, people will look. When our girls make every attempt to show that they are developing into young women, wearing their tops just as low as they possibly can, people will be looking.

As far as our boys go, what is the attraction of wearing jeans and shorts half way down their legs? If they desire to show their undies that badly, maybe they could simply not wear pants or shorts. Do they honestly think they look cool? What a painfully silly and embarrassing lie! What we wear can be a direct reflection of our hearts. Proverbs 4:23 states, "Above all else, guard your heart, for it is the wellspring of life."

Sadly, the incredible growth of child pornography goes hand in hand with our children's dress and what is perceived as acceptable.

Dear ones, God loves us so very much and He truly knows what is best for us and for our children. Even though we may not understand everything about Him, WE CAN FULLY TRUST HIM!! You can raise G rated kids in an R rated world. Without a doubt, it takes more time and effort to do so, but the rewards are phenomenal.

Seeds of Encouragement

Galatians 6:7 says, "Do not be deceived: God cannot be mocked. A man reaps what he sows." What an incredible promise! Our efforts in raising our kids according to God's design do not come back void. You will be blessed and so will they.

Take heart and take the time. And by our example in thought, word and deed, may the whole world know that Jesus loves us so!

Seeds of Encouragement

God desires that EVERY corner of our hearts and minds belong to Him. Children are especially vulnerable to the lies of our culture. By using Deuteronomy 6:5-9 as our parenting road map, our path will have fewer bumps, potholes and detours.

"Adolescence is perhaps nature's way of preparing parents to welcome the empty nest."
Karen Savage and Patricia Adams

Got Teens?

"You've got to be kidding me Mom!" Exasperated again by something I said or did, my teenager sighed heavily and looked at me as if I had a celery stalk growing out of my head. His furrowed brow and squinty eyes said it all! I simply didn't understand his position. How could I? It must have been the Stone Age when I was a teenager, or at least it might as well be from his perspective.

I'm teen challenged. I readily admit my weakness. I know I need help with the complex set of issues one encounters when raising teens. I've been thinking seriously of starting a support group. I just know there are other parents out there like me. I went to college and have a career, yet every day it seems like I get dumber and dumber in my teen's eyes. My husband and I are thinking about getting t-shirts that say, "I'm with stupid." That way when people see us out in the community, they'll have no expectations of us. They'll already know we're steadily losing brain cells and before long we won't be able to concurrently talk and walk.

Schools are always looking for effective fundraisers. I believe I have the answer: selling shirts, banners, coffee mugs and miniature footballs with the letters ITC (short for "I'm Teen Challenged") emblazoned boldly on them. What parents wouldn't support that cause? We all suffer from the same quizzical looks, muttered comments, raised arms and the ever so famous question, "Are you serious??!!"

When we see each other on the street or at school functions with our ITC memorabilia no words will have to be spoken. We will automatically know the frustrations we're each feeling. We'll hug, sigh and encourage one another to continue the good fight. Knowing that ITC doesn't last forever and someday, yes someday, we will regain our intelligence. These dark days won't last forever.

So...for those brave souls who along with me are teen challenged, be encouraged. Joshua 1:9 states, "Have I not commanded you? Be strong and courageous. Do not be terrified; do not be discouraged, for the LORD your God will be with you wherever you go."

There you have it...we're not alone. Whatever teen challenges you're having today, hold fast! You're going to make it!

Seeds of Encouragement

Are you teen challenged today? Be encouraged! Raising kids is a lot like going on a river trip. Sometimes the waters are calm and peaceful, other times the rivers foam with such intensity that our hearts pound and make us question if we're on the right course. But when we come to the end of our river adventure, we breathe a sigh and realize what an incredible thrill it's been!

"When you're down to nothing, God is up to something.
The faithful see the invisible, believe the incredible
and then receive the impossible."

John F. Murray

Hope Floats

"Teens today are so irresponsible, unpredictable; they don't know their heads from a hole in the ground." Ever heard (or made) those comments before?

Teens are definitely in a world of their own sometimes. After pouring milk into his morning cereal, my 15 year old Clay has opened the pantry door and placed the gallon of milk on a shelf right beside the cereal. Research shows that the frontal lobe of their brains, which is where planning, judgment and reasoning reside, is not fully developed until they're 23 years old. I guess I should expect to find milk in the pantry sometimes!

Their cell phones seem to be as natural a part of their bodies are as the hair on their heads. They're hormonal, impulsive, and irrational. They are convinced that money simply appears whenever they need it. But for all the stress that can ensue with them, there are times that teens are simply amazing!

Recently my friend Kristin told me that she had lost her cell phone at a family recreational site. Being a smart phone she had her bank information, passwords, contacts, memorable pictures and many other items stored on it. She quickly began scanning each area of the site for her phone, asking employees for help and other patrons as well. Coming across a group of teenage girls by the pool, she asked them too if they had seen her phone. Looking obviously uncomfortable, they all said they hadn't seen it. Kristen knew they looked suspicious and felt in her heart that they indeed had her phone. She asked them again. They still said, "No." But having no proof, she and her family left for home.

A couple days later her husband called her at home. "Your phone is in the mail and will be here soon," he said. "What?!" Kristen exclaimed. Her husband went on to tell her the whole story. One of the girls that Kristen had spoken to in the group by the pool had gone to church with her mom on Sunday. While at church she became so convicted of stealing the phone, she confessed the entire thing to her mom. Her mom called Kristen's husband who was listed on her phone and asked for their address. That week Kristen got her phone back unscathed.

Yesterday, I was taping a segment with a successful motivational speaker from North Carolina. I was nervous and hoping I wouldn't flub it up! While I was preparing, my nephew Zac came over to visit. I was scurrying around, checking and rechecking some items. Zac, being the comic he is, was jokingly harassing me about my segment. "Don't put that there. What if you sneeze during your taping? What are you going to wear? What if the dogs bark the whole time? I think I'll come over and make faces at you while you're taping!" I fired back, "Don't you even think about coming over, Zacarack!" (my nickname for him),"I'm nervous enough!"

The morning of the taping I got up early and began getting ready. While eating breakfast I received a text from Zac. It read "Morning, Auntie! Hey, I just wanted to wish you good luck today with that guy. Don't think of him as someone higher than you Auntie, just think of him as a teammate because you are both playing for the same team, brothers in Christ and want the same positive outcome. He just has a little more playing time and you can learn from his experiences. Hope it goes well! Love you, Zacarack"

I was blown away! Wisdom beyond his years and truth as solid as it comes!

So yes, teenagers are absent minded, immature, head strong and moody. But sometimes they give us those glimmers of optimism. A great conversation or moments of laughter together are so encouraging to those embroiled in the teen years.

Be encouraged! Don't give up! The next time you find yourself discouraged with your teen and you wonder if there's any hope, read this again. When all else fails, hope floats.

Seeds of Encouragement

I love teenagers! I remember my younger days so vividly; days that could bring me to the height of exhilaration and to the depths of despair within a few short hours or even minutes. Teenagers have a lot going on in their heads, hearts and bodies. We need to be patient with them. They'll get there. We just need to give them some time.

Blessed Are the Days

Boys climbing trees,
Chatting endlessly,
Blessed are the days such as these.

Bare feet in the grass,
Cats scampering past,
Blessed are the days such as these.

Thump of ball bouncing,
Whirl of bats swinging,
Blessed are the days such as these.

Jingle of doorbells ringing,
Shrill of children screaming,
Blessed are the days such as these.

Sweet, butterfly kisses,
Dirt streaked, smiling faces,
Blessed are the days such as these.

Moments flutter by,
Time seems to fly,
Thank you Lord for days such as these.

Andrea Sharp

Holidays/Seasons

"And so, my fellow Americans: ask not what your country can do for you - ask what you can do for your country."

John F. Kennedy

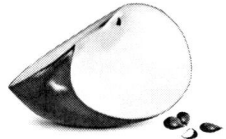

I love the different seasons and the holidays that come with each one! Celebrating with family, friends and food is always at the top of my holiday list. Holidays are celebrations that bring people together. Building relationships and connecting with others is a wonderful gift from God. Enjoy your celebrations, whether big or small. The time together makes memories for a lifetime.

Independence Day

"In my anguish I cried to the LORD, and he answered by setting me free. The LORD is with me; I will not be afraid. What can man do to me? The LORD is with me; he is my helper." Psalm 118: 5-7

I dropped my luggage on the hotel floor. I had been traveling for over 14 hours. I was exhausted and spent. It was just after midnight on the East coast. I had left my boys behind at the airport and with tear-streaked cheeks boarded my flight. I would be training in Virginia for the next week for a new teaching position. I had never been away from my crew for that length of time.

I sighed heavily as I thought of not seeing their adorable faces for a week. I dug deep into my overstuffed suitcase and pulled out my family photo. The picture made me smile. I turned on my phone to call and let Matt know I had arrived. My voicemail showed four missed messages, three from Matt and one from my sister Jackie.

I knew it was strange for Matt to call that many times. He's not one who likes to chat idly on the phone. After he found out I'd made it ok he asked, "Have you spoken to Jackie yet?" "No, I haven't," I said, "What's going on?" He answered, "They've found a mass in her colon and it doesn't look good."

Details were sketchy as Matt had not spoken to her directly but had gotten bits of information from other family members. I didn't want to jump to conclusions until I spoke to Jackie. I wanted to hear from her what was said and how doctors were going to proceed.

The next three days were incredibly draining. I was on information overload with training and when I wasn't in conferences, I was on the phone with Jackie and family getting updates. Jackie called me on Wednesday night. Her voice was heavy as she relayed the news. The mass was cancerous, inoperable and terminal. I sat stunned. Words didn't come. I was dumbfounded. How could something like this happen so quickly, for someone so young?

In quiet times, I went to the Lord. Friends I had just met surrounded me with love, comfort and group prayer. It was incredibly difficult concentrating during training and I pondered coming home early.

One of my 'default settings' is fear. "I don't understand Lord," I said to God over and over. He continued to remind me of His sovereignty. Psalm 112:7-8 says, "He will have no fear of bad news; his heart is steadfast, trusting in the LORD. His heart is secure; he will have no fear..." "Lord, I don't want to fear, I want to trust. Please help me," I prayed.

Much to our disbelief, Jackie passed away ten days later, three days after her 45th birthday. A devoted mother, she left behind a handsome, well-mannered and intelligent 14 year old son. It was a complete shock for all of us!

My sister Jackie was a Navy veteran and as Independence Day draws near, I realize I never thanked her for her dedication in ensuring my liberty. She was in the first Gulf War and stationed just outside of Iraq. My dad was in the army and my brother-in-law is a retired Marine. I owe the freedom I enjoy each day to them and those of the armed services, past and present. I am forever in debt to them for the freedom they have fought to ensure.

Matthew 10:8 states, "Freely you have received, freely give." God in His incredible mercies has blessed us in this country with so many gifts and opportunities. We have independence because of those who have given up their freedoms and families, sacrificing everything for you and me.

Seeds of Encouragement

This Independence Day, I want to say THANK YOU to all military personnel. I know your sacrifice, as well as your family's, has been great. "Greater love has no one than this, that he lay down his life for his friends." (John 15:13) Jesus spoke this to teach His friends and disciples about His love for them and what he would do as a demonstration of sacrificial love by giving up His life on the cross.

Dear friends, freedom is NEVER FREE! Take time to say thank you to God today for the freedom you have in Him. Say thank you to those who have given everything for the love of our country.

Independence Day ~ Let us rejoice in the land of the free and the home of the brave!

Seeds of Encouragement

God has given me such a heart for our military. For so little, they give so much! To military personnel and their families I salute you for what you've given to me! I can never begin to thank you enough. Friends, let's show our deep respect and honor for those who have so freely sacrificed for us.

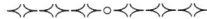

"Jesus answered, 'I am the way and the truth and the life. No one comes to the Father except through me.'"

John 14:6

Jesus ~ Trick? Or Treat?

Jesus: Son of God, Holy of Holies, the Bright Morning Star, Man of Sorrows, Great Shepherd, the Only Begotten Son

Trick: A crafty practice or procedure meant to deceive or defraud

Treat: To pay another's expenses, an unexpected source of joy or delight

What is Jesus to you? Is He a famous teacher, an example of how to live a good life? Is He your lifeline when things are tumultuous, a figure on a wooden cross? Or is He more; your everything, your rock, your hope, your very salvation?

For years I went about life knowing who Jesus was but never letting Him have a full effect on my attitudes and actions. I was a talker, but not a walker. I loved God, but was selfish and full of wants. As long as Jesus didn't conflict with my own agenda, I was happy. Or so I thought! What God eventually melted into my heart (once I allowed it), was the fact that giving up on how I wanted to live, and submitting to God's plan for me, provided me with the freedom and peace I'd always longed for.

So...who is Jesus to you? Has He made a decisive impact on your life, attitudes and actions? Does His reflection shine in you? Or is He merely a historical or religious figure, whom you recognize, but with no lingering effect?

Jesus was either the most influential person who has ever walked the earth, or He is the biggest maniac history has ever known. John 14:6 says, "Jesus answered, 'I am the way and the truth and the life. No one comes to the Father except through me.'" Romans 1:19 states, "Since what may be known about God is plain to them, because GOD HAS MADE IT PLAIN TO THEM. For since the creation of the world God's invisible qualities - his eternal power and divine nature - have been clearly seen, being understood from what has been made, SO THAT MEN ARE WITHOUT EXCUSE." (Emphasis mine) "For even the Son of Man did not come to be served, but to serve, and to give his life as a ransom for many." Mark 10:45

A great preacher named Dr. Shadrach Meshach Lockridge, in his message, "That's My King!" has these things to say about who Jesus is:

> He's the king of righteousness. He's the king of the ages. He's the king of heaven. He's the king of glory. He's the king of kings. He's enduringly strong. He's entirely sincere. He's eternally steadfast. He's immortally graceful. He's infinitely powerful. He's impartially merciful. Do you know Him? He's the greatest phenomenon that has ever crossed the horizon of this world. He's God's Son.
>
> He's the sinner's Savior. He's the centerpiece of civilization. He stands in the solitude of Himself. He's honest and He's unique. He's unparalleled. He's unprecedented. He supplies strength for the weak. He's available for the tempted and tried. He sympathizes and He saves. He strengthens and sustains. He guards and He guides. He heals the sick. He cleanses the leper. He forgives the sinner. He discharges debtors. He delivers the captive. He defends the feeble. He blesses the young. He serves the unfortunate. He regards the aged. He rewards the diligent. And He beautifies the meek. I wonder if you know Him.

Oh, beloved, do you KNOW Him or do you know about Him? This day, realize, accept and embrace the gift of life He offers you. It's not a trick, a lie or deceit. Jesus is the real deal!

Seeds of Encouragement

Dear one, who is Jesus to you? Has He made a decisive impact on your life, attitudes and actions? Does His reflection shine in you? Or is He merely a historical or religious figure, whom you recognize, but has had no lingering effect? His arms are open wide ready to receive your heart today. I encourage you not to delay, for we know not what tomorrow brings.

Center of our Celebration

Winter celebrations are abundant around our home. Thanksgiving Day falls on the last Thursday of November. My parent's anniversary is in the first week of December. My mom's birthday is December 23rd. Another family member's birthday is December 24th and the birthday of Jesus is celebrated on the 25th. My birthday happens to fall on the 27th. By that time no one has any energy or money, and we're all tired of celebrating. Woe is me! They're probably gearing up for New Year's Eve!

I'm a fanatic for birthdays! I absolutely love them! It's a day all about that person. You're the center of the celebration. My family knows this full well. I enjoy hearing, "Happy birthday!" from dawn till dusk; being greeted with breakfast in bed and knowing I'm the birthday girl all day long! I bask in the attention!

One year, my sweet husband, God bless him, decided to combine Christmas with my birthday. That did not go over well and he has never done that again. Now we go up to the mountains each year, rent a cabin and frolic in the snow for a few days. My day is separate. My boys are fully aware of my passion for birthdays. Even after my birthday, they'll say, "Happy belated birthday, Mom!" or "Hope you had a good birthday!"

This afternoon I got to thinking: God, in His infinite wisdom knew exactly when I needed to be born. It's good my birthday falls on December 27th. With the way I love the attention birthdays give, it's a good thing I'm not a June baby. I'd probably want to celebrate for a least a week! But the real attention needs to be focused on one thing only; Jesus, the Son of God, our Savior. In John 8:12, Jesus states, "I am the light of the world." He is the center of absolutely everything, even birthdays.

Seeds of Encouragement

This month we have celebrated two more birthdays in our family. Each one lasted three glorious, fun filled days! We're exhausted, but we had a good time!

Beloved, whether you're celebrating the sun coming up over the mountains, butterfly kisses from your little ones, or a loved one's birthday, make Jesus the center of the celebration. It's all about Him anyway! No matter what a day may bring, it's still all about Jesus. He is indeed the center of it all!!

Seeds of Encouragement

I love celebrations! The food, fellowship and music joined together can bring tremendous joy! When God is at the center of our celebrations He gets the opportunity to rejoice along with us. Heaven and earth rejoicing together? Now that's a party!

"Christmas is not a time nor a season, but a state of mind. To cherish peace and goodwill, to be plenteous in mercy, is to have the real spirit of Christmas."

Calvin Coolidge

Face it, Trace It and Erase It

The sweet smell of banana nut bread filled the air. My boys, big and small, came to ask what was baking. Everyone eagerly waited for the timer to finish so that we could partake of this delicacy.

Anyone who knows me, realizes that I am NOT Betty Crocker. Cooking is not something that comes easily to me, although I do try. I want to be a good cook, but the talent escapes me. My family readily realizes this. So for them to comment one by one on how good my bread smelled was quite a treat for me!

55 minutes later, the timer dinged and everyone rushed to the oven waiting for me to take the banana nut bread out. When I opened the oven, much to our dismay, instead of seeing a loaf of dessert, our eyes looked upon a gooey blob. The loaf had no solidity. Everyone squinted and tried to figure out exactly what this was because it certainly wasn't bread. "What's wrong with it Mom?" "It's so gooey!" "Does this mean we can't have any?" What was the problem, I asked myself. What went wrong? My husband Matt, who is always the voice of reason, said, "Did you put in all of the ingredients?"

"Did I put in all of the ingredients? Of course, I did!" I snapped. To show him the foolishness of his question, I immediately went to my *Betty Crocker* cookbook and began reading each ingredient out loud. "Sugar, butter, eggs, bananas, water, baking soda, salt, flour..." A long pause ensued. Flour, how could I forget the FLOUR??? It's the main part, with the exception of the bananas! Aaargh!!

My Betty Crocker moment was gone in a flash! We all were looking forward to tasting this sweet morsel. My intentions were good, but my actions proved otherwise. Banana nut bread simply doesn't work without flour, no matter what else I put in.

As we enter this Christmas season, I have spoken with many who are facing difficulty in one area or another in their lives. People who are discouraged, distracted and disheartened. Today I want to bring your focus back to the One who is the healer of our souls and the provider for our needs.

The simplicity of Jesus and His undying, never ending love for you is the focal point. When it is all said and done, Jesus and His devotion to us is the only thing that never changes. Money, possessions, family and friends come and go throughout our lives, but the story of the Son of God, coming to earth, to show us the very face of God is always the same. God's Word, the Bible, does NOT change! In James 1:17, it says that our Father "does not change like shifting shadows." Malachi 3:6 states, "I the LORD do not change."

Beloved, my point is this: Without Jesus as the focal point of your heart and mind this Christmas, you're going to end up like my banana bread: great intentions, but mushy and unable to hold together.

Remember our adversary comes to steal, kill and destroy. If he can keep you thinking about your circumstances versus the goodness of God, then he is glad and victorious. We need to remember that the victory is ours as children of God. James 4:7 states, "Resist the devil and he will flee from you." It goes on to say "Come near to God and he will come near to you." (Verse 8) We have the power to rebuke our enemy and God's Word says he has to flee! That is a great promise and we can use it with full authority!

Seeds of Encouragement

Years ago on *Saturday Night Live*, the actors performed a skit in which they repeated these words: "Face it, trace it and erase it!" Friends, I say those same words to you today. Face whatever it is that ails your heart and mind, and bring it to God. Trace the reason for the circumstances. If it's something you have done to cause a problem, then go and rectify the situation or relationship. (Remember, love means always having to say you're sorry.) If the situation is not something you can control, lay that issue at the feet of Jesus, ask Him to handle it and trust Him with the results. Then erase it; meaning give it over fully to God. Confess your sins to God and let it go! Stewing over circumstances that we wish were different doesn't change anything other than our blood pressure.

"Trust in the LORD with all your heart and lean NOT ON YOUR OWN UNDERSTANDING; IN ALL YOUR WAYS ACKNOWLEDGE HIM, and he will make your paths straight." Proverbs 3:5-6 (Emphasis mine)

Sadly, beloved, I know from whence I speak. I have faced much heartache, pain and loss. I know what it's like to look to people, circumstances and stuff to bring me joy and contentment. It simply doesn't work. Ask yourself this: If I lost everything and everyone in my circle, would I still find peace in God alone? "When peace like a river, attends my way, When sorrows like sea billows roll; whatever my lot, thou has taught me to say, It is well, it is well with my soul." ("It Is Well With My Soul", Horatio G. Spafford) Whatever your lot, dear soul, you need to keep your eyes and heart on the One who supplies "peace that surpasses understanding". (Philippians 4:7)

For you and me, this can be the best Christmas ever! Whatever it is today that takes your eyes off of God: Face it, trace it and erase it! Stand on God's love and His promises. The simplicity of the Christmas story and a king who gave up everything, so that we may know that Jesus loves us so, is what it is all about.   Merry Christmas!

Seeds of Encouragement

"Trust in the LORD with all your heart and lean not on your own understanding; in all your ways acknowledge him, and he will make your paths straight." Proverbs 3:5-6. Sometimes it can be hard to keep our eyes on God. He knows that, beloved. But a peaceful heart comes from laying down our own perception and picking up trust in its place, over and over again until it's engrained in our hearts.

"The star of Bethlehem was a star of hope that led the wise men to the fulfillment of their expectations, the success of their expedition. Nothing in this world is more fundamental for success in life than hope, and this star pointed to our only source for true hope: Jesus Christ"

D. James Kennedy

Believe God

Wouldn't life be so much simpler if we just believed God? What if we took Him at His Word and believed His promises?

For years, I've wanted a Christmas wreath that said simply "Believe God."

I called Shelley at Shelley's Gifts on Olive Avenue and put in my request. Knowing her knack for making the simple beautiful, I asked if she could make this wreath for me. In a couple of days, she presented me with a gorgeous wreath that frames my door. In bright red letters it says, 'Believe God'. In between the words she placed a cross with a gem in the middle. It's stunning!

Believing God…why is that so hard for us? Throughout the Bible God gives us promises that we can rely on and claim every single day. "Never will I leave you; never will I forsake you." (Hebrews 13:5) Forsake means give up. God will NEVER give you up! **Believe God.**

"Trust in the LORD with all your heart and lean not on your own understanding; in all your ways acknowledge him, and he will make your paths straight." (Proverbs 3:5-6) **Believe God.**

"For God so loved the world (the world is you and me) that he gave his one and only son, that whoever believes in him shall NOT perish but have eternal life." (John 3:16 – emphasis mine) **Believe God.**

"Do not be anxious about ANYTHING, but in EVERYTHING, by prayer and petition, WITH THANKSGIVING, present your requests to God. And the peace of God, which TRANSCENDS ALL UNDERSTANDING, will guard your hearts and your minds in Christ Jesus. (Philippians 3:6-7 emphasis mine) **Believe God.**

Seeds of Encouragement

"He gives strength to the weary and increases the power of the weak…but those who hope (wait) in the LORD will renew their strength." (Isaiah 40:29, 31a) **Believe God.**

"For I know the plans I have for you," declares the LORD, "plans to prosper you and not to harm you, plans to give you hope and a future. Then you will call upon me and come and pray to me, and I will listen to you. You will seek me and find me when you seek me with all your heart." (Jeremiah 29:11-13) **Believe God.**

"Come to me, all you who are weary and burdened, and I will give you rest. " (Matthew 11:28) **Believe God.**

"And there were shepherds living out in the fields nearby, keeping watch over their flocks at night. An angel of the Lord appeared to them, and the glory of the Lord shone around them, and they were terrified. But the angel said to them, 'Do not be afraid. I bring you good news that will cause great joy for all the people. Today in the town of David **a Savior has been born to you; he is the Messiah, the Lord.** This will be a sign to you: You will find a baby wrapped in cloths and lying in a manger.' Suddenly a great company of the heavenly host appeared with the angel, praising God and saying, 'Glory to God in the highest heaven, and on earth peace to those on whom his favor rests.'" (Luke 2:8-14) **Believe God.**

As we celebrate Christmas and ring in the New Year, believe God! His promises are true and forever! His Word applies to us all, no matter where we're at or what we've done. **Believe God.**

Seeds of Encouragement

Sometimes it can be hard to wrap our heads around believing so completely in something we can't see. That's where faith comes in. We believe there's air all around us even though we can't see it. We see the results of the air; oxygen to breathe, leaves moving in the trees and or feeling a breeze on our face. God's presence is visible as well. The sun comes up in the east each morning and we have the moon as our night light. Babies live in their mother's womb breathing fluid and after they're born they breathe air. What if we took God at His Word and believed what He said? Life changing results would be inevitable!

For the Sake of the Call

I was facing a dilemma: white chocolate mocha or mocha chip frappe? Short, tall, venti, grande, half-caf, decaf, nonfat, low-fat or soy?

I was alone in the Dallas/Fort Worth airport. I could order whatever I wanted and not share a single drop, so my decision needed to be just right. With three growing boys, I rarely taste anything without being asked for a bite or a sip. So with this rare opportunity before me I wanted to savor each and every drop. I could almost taste the sweet drink that would soon be solely mine.

The coffee café just happened to be next to the boarding gate I needed to get on. While in line I noticed two young military men sitting and waiting for the same flight. My heart was immediately drawn to them. After getting my coffee I stood near the two men and began watching the news on a megatron television screen that took up an entire wall. News from around the globe was transmitting loud and clear.

As people waited for flights and mingled through the corridors, many would glance up at the humongous screen. Occasionally I would glance over at those young men and wonder where they were going and where they'd been.

The news on the megatron centered on the economy, joblessness, and what retailers were predicting financially from Christmas shoppers.

My heart kept returning to the young military men. An opportunity was before me and I had to take it. I walked over to one of them and introduced myself. "Hi, I'm Andrea," I said as I put out my hand. He looked at me, shook my hand, and said, "Hi," ever so softly. "I just wanted to tell you how much I appreciate your service and what you do to serve me and my family. I'm so thankful for you." I said. He blinked and shyly said, "Thank you ma'am."

Seeds of Encouragement

I went back to where I was standing and continued watching the news, killing time until my flight. The news anchor began discussing aspects of the war in Afghanistan. She cited a new Gallup poll in which it showed the support for the war there was at an all time low. "Oh, Lord," I prayed, "please don't let those guys hear this report. Just block their ears from hearing it. I don't want them to feel like their duty is in vain." I turned to see if they were watching. One was listening to his headset and the other was reading. I continued to lift them up to God that they would not hear any of the news story.

My flight number was called and I joined the procession to board. Once I was on the plane I began looking for my seat. I knew mine was beside the window, and I began looking for it. Row 22, alas. Two men were already seated. As I made my way back I saw that the person who I would be sitting right next to was one of the military men who I stood by at the gate. A couple behind our row was already asking him where he was going and where he'd been. I shook his hand and introduced myself. He was returning for a three week vacation to see his family in Fresno. He had just finished basic training in Arkansas. He looked tired, but he was clearly excited about going home.

A flight attendant walked up and spoke directly to him. "We have an extra seat in first class. Would you like it?" The young man smiled and put his head down. The other man in our row said, "Take it man, you can't beat first class." "You deserve it!" the couple behind us said. Slowly, he rose and began to get up. An eruption of clapping began by a few, I joined in and everyone on the airplane began to clap and cheer. Tears began to well up in my eyes. God quietly whispered in my heart, "Gallup polls or not Andrea, I'm taking care of these men." "Oh thank you, God." I cried as I continued to clap and cheer.

"Greater love has no one than this, that he lay down his life for his friends." John 15:13

Seeds of Encouragement

When we got to baggage claim in Fresno this man was enveloped in the arms of a young woman and two little girls. Home sweet home.

With both Veteran's Day and Thanksgiving this month, may we all express our sincere appreciation for those who have served and continue to serve us. May we honor, pray for and encourage our military and their families.

May God continue to bless this great land of the United States of America! Let's remember the freedoms we enjoy are because of the sacrifice of young men and women who have decided in their hearts that we're worth everything they have to offer, even life itself. All for the sake of the call.

Seeds of Encouragement

Coming from a military family I am keenly aware of the sacrifice our military makes for me and the rest of our great country.
Freedom has never been free. It's a gift that's been bestowed upon us by incredible men and women.
I am so very thankful for their service to my family and the sacrifice of themselves that they so readily provide to us!

My Forever Love
A Father's Day Tribute

"Bye Dad." "I love you!" "We'll see you soon." I said softly as we settled him in the front seat of our car. My husband Matt was taking Dad (my father-in-law) back to his home in Fresno.

They drove out of the driveway and down the road. I breathed a long sigh of relief. We had brought Dad home for 3 days, back to where he'd lived for the past 8 years. Readjusting back to our home proved much more difficult than we had anticipated. Fresno was Dad's home now and he was happy there.

While Dad was with us, Matt slept each night on the couch beside his bed, because at 93 Dad sometimes gets confused when he wakes up in the night. Three weeks prior Dad had had surgery. The surgery was a difficult process and Dad wasn't gaining strength back very quickly. He looked feeble and frail. He was pale and often light headed.

Matt got little sleep as Dad had severe pain in his hips and legs. Matt would massage his joints, resituate him on his bed and place pillows under and beside him.

When morning came Matt went to work and I took over. Breakfast and bath were on my agenda for Dad. Both were complete failures. Dad almost passed out three different times, his catheter began leaking, and holding him up proved much more difficult than I imagined. Soon I was in tears. My sister came to help and 3 hours later we were fixing breakfast. "I'm in way over my head." I cried to my sister, "We can't do this alone!"

Dad couldn't be left alone at all. He required 24 hour, minute by minute care and attention. Family and friends came to help us, and others brought meals.

Seeds of Encouragement

The next day Matt stayed with Dad while I went to work. Before I left I came in to Dad's room. There was Matt lovingly sponge bathing Dad, limb by limb. After he washed an area, he would gently massage lotion onto his dry skin. Step by step, time after time, Matt would repeat this process until Dad was washed and dressed.

Being Dad's youngest, Matt was now in the role of lovingly fathering his own father. Sleeping next to his bed so he wouldn't be afraid, massaging his aches and pains, bathing, dressing and feeding his dad were all necessary components to his care.

As I write this I'm filled with tremendous love and gratitude for Matt. I want him to know that every gentle act he does is recorded and seen by our heavenly Father who is incredibly proud of how he's served his parents, his sons and me.

Matt has led by example. Actions are always heard much louder than words ever could be. The way he's always loved me is teaching his sons the role of a good husband and faithful companion.

I've seen the countless baseball pitches he's caught in the backyard, the wrestling matches he's engaged in when it's been 3 boys to one dad and all the times he's played king of the mountain in the swimming pool. Reading stories to our sons, doing daily Bible reading and prayer with them have engrained lifelong values in their hearts and minds forever.

I am eternally grateful for Matt. He is my forever love! I'm so very proud of the daddy he is and the man he's become as he's sought to seek the Lord each day. This Father's Day I salute you, Matt, and all the other dads who have sacrificed so much in a multitude of ways. We appreciate you so very much!

Happy Father's Day!

Seeds of Encouragement

Fatherhood can be a taxing, draining and sometimes thankless job. Take a moment to show appreciation to your father or a father you know. Send a note of thanksgiving, jot down a special memory or appreciation for their efforts. Being a good dad isn't for the faint of heart. Dads need to hear we take notice of all they do. Thank you to all the fathers who give so much love, time and attention!

Memories Made

"Life gives us brief moments with another...but sometimes in those brief moments we get memories that last a lifetime..."

Author Unknown

In making memories, last October, we were headed to our school's Fall Festival. It's a wonderful event with hay rides, game booths, pictures, food and tons of sweets. Before we left home I was kicking myself for not thinking ahead. This year I wanted it to be different. I wanted so badly to enjoy the fun alongside my boys and dress up too!

A thought occurred to me that there might be something in my closet I could quickly alter and make into some sort of costume-looking attire. I hurriedly scanned my clothes, peeking at this and looking at that. Everything was just too plain and I had no time for creativity. Just then something caught my eye. What was that in the back corner? Lo and behold, it was my high school cheerleading outfit.

I pulled it out and gave it a good look. "There's no way I'm getting into this thing!" I said out loud. Giving birth to three children and my love for pizza determined that! But the longer I gazed at it, the more I thought, "Well...maybe." Plus, I read the fabric type and it was made of a material called 'Orlon'. It looked like it would possibly, with any luck, stretch.

With a whim and a prayer I squeezed into the sweater. It was tight! My chest felt like it was being compressed in a vise and the sleeves were so snug I had trouble raising my arms. But victory was mine! I was completely shocked that something I hadn't worn for almost 30 years STILL fit! Tight, no less, but I had it on. My name and year of graduation were still clearly visible on the front. I fondly whispered, "It's been a long time." With a sigh and a smile I joined my two younger sons for Halloween costume pictures. A glorious moment indeed!

Seeds of Encouragement

My 14 year old son, Clay, had already gone to the festival to assist with the game booths. Together with our other two sons, Jaden and Landon, I drove to the festival. I couldn't contain my glee! I smiled at each attendee, rejoicing in the awe that I was sure everyone would share with me in seeing my authentic outfit. We slowly made our way through game booths. Jaden and Landon were filling their stomachs with sweets at each successive game. Finally, we arrived at Clay's booth. He was busy handing out candy to lucky recipients who shot the basketball in the hoop.

When it was our turn, I quickly walked up to Clay and gave him a hug. "Look at this son! I have on my high school cheerleading sweater! Can you believe it?!" I squealed with delight! "Wow, mom!" Clay replied. My thrill was evident, "I know! Pretty cool, huh?" I said confidently. With a quizzical look, Clay replied, "You must have been pretty big in high school." My jaw dropped and my back stiffened. For a moment I seriously considered stuffing him in the basketball hoop! Choosing the high road, I thought better of it. My burning glare made him rethink his statement. As I turned and huffed away, I could hear him hollering, "Mom, that didn't come out right!" My moment of sheer delight was shattered in an instant!

I get a kick out of this memory now. My son and I have both learned from it. He's learning to engage his brain before speaking and I have learned to be careful when seeking opinions from teenagers. They're much too forthright!

This fall with the coming holidays, traditions and celebrations I pray the memories you make are spectacular! Whether they bring a tear to your eye or a lift in your step, just remember memories are made for a purpose; teaching, guiding and enabling us to be all that we've been created for.

Seeds of Encouragement

Memories pull at our heart strings. Memories can make us laugh, feel embarrassed or make us cry. Our life is made up of the memories we've made and are continuing to make. Life travels fast and opportunities fade. Take some time today to make a wonderful memory. Looking back you'll certainly be glad you did!